THE INSIDE STORY OF THE
STATE QUARTERS

A Behind-the-Scenes Look at America's Favorite New Coins

Q. DAVID BOWERS

CREDITS AND ACKNOWLEDGEMENTS

Whitman Publishing, LLC, and the author express appreciation to the following people who provided information or helped in other ways for this book and/or for the forthcoming larger book upon which it is based, tentatively titled *A Guide Book of Washington and State-Reverse Quarter Dollars*:

Stephen M. Bieda • Garrett and Michelle Burke • Greg Burns • Donald D. Carlucci • Terry Campbell • G.C. Carnes • Daniel Carr • The Commission of Fine Arts, Washington, DC • Beth Deisher • Gloria Eskridge (United States Mint) • Howard Feltham • Bill Fivaz • Henrietta Holsman Fore (former director of the United States Mint) • Roberta A. French • Charles H. Hosch • Paul Jackson • Jay Johnson (former director of the United States Mint) • Cynthia Meals (United States Mint) • John Mercanti (U.S. Mint sculptor-engraver) • Michele Orzano • Spencer Peck • Alex Shagin • Mark Smith • Thomas Snyder • Don K. Stout • Rick Snow • David M. Sundman • Garland Travis • The United States Mint • Frank Van Valen • Eric von Klinger • Ben Weinstein • Frank Wight

In addition, news articles, letters, and other reports published in *Coin World, COINage, Coins* magazine, *Numismatic News*, and *Numismatist* were of great help, as well as other periodicals (as noted in the text).

The text, by Q. David Bowers, is excerpted and modified from a forthcoming Whitman Publishing book tentatively titled *A Guide Book of Washington and State-Reverse Quarter Dollars*.

Non-quarter coin photographs (of commemorative half dollars, colonial tokens, etc.) are courtesy of the *Guide Book of United States Coins* (Whitman Publishing, 2005). Illustrations are from the author's historical image archives.

For a complete catalog of numismatic reference books, supplies, and storage products, visit Whitman Publishing online at www.whitmanbooks.com.

STATE QUARTERS:
SINCE 1999, EVERYBODY HAS BEEN TALKING ABOUT THEM!

Today, these wonderful state-reverse quarter dollars have captured the attention and interest of just about everyone. Serious collectors, or *numismatists*, strive to obtain a specimen of each, in brilliant Mint State or Proof finish. Millions of other people—regular citizens—eagerly check their pocket change to see what's new, to find a coin honoring New Jersey, California, Alabama, or another state, minted from 1999 to present, or to see for the first time the latest release.

Each year the United States Mint issues five new designs, each featuring a different state, in the order in which the states joined the Union. In the pages to follow you will learn all about these fascinating coins—remarkable in their diversity, unequalled in their historical importance, and inexpensive enough that anyone can afford to collect them.

ABOUT THE STATE QUARTER PROGRAM

THE UNITED STATES MINT

As a bit of background, beginning with the new commemorative coin program launched by Mint Director Donna Pope in 1982, the Bureau of the Mint (as it was then called) went into high gear with innovative marketing concepts. Since then, many different and interesting Proof and commemorative sets have been offered in various purchase options.

Similarly, since the inception of the state quarters program in 1999, the Mint has been creative, and along the way new ideas have been implemented, among the most recent being the offering of small 100-coin bags of individual issues, 1,000-coin bags, and rolls. From a financial and popularity viewpoint, the entire program has been a spectacular success.

The United States Mint has done much in its outreach to collectors in recent decades. This includes the administrations of Mint directors Philip Diehl, Jay Johnson, and Henrietta Holsman Fore (who left the post in August 2005) during the quarters program from 1999 to date, and is likely to continue under successive directors. Collectors and writers have been warmly welcomed, exhibits have been mounted at coin conventions, and much information has been supplied to numismatic periodicals.

THE STATE QUARTER PROGRAM

In 1999, the United States Mint launched the 50 State Quarters® Program. Its premise: each year five states of the Union would suggest designs for the reverse of the quarter dollar, the motifs to depict some aspect of state history, tradition, nature, or fame. Each quarter would be released in the order its state joined the Union, launched by an appropriate ceremony attended by Mint officials and dignitaries. These launches

would be spaced throughout the year—roughly one new coin design every 10 weeks. Coins for circulation would be struck at the Philadelphia and Denver mints, while Proof versions would be struck for collectors at the San Francisco Mint, in clad composition as well as silver.

OBVERSE CHANGES

In 1999, to accommodate the creative designs intended for the reverse of the state quarters, the inscriptions UNITED STATES OF AMERICA and QUARTER DOLLAR were relocated to the obverse (the "front" or "face" of the coin), above and below the portrait, respectively. LIBERTY and IN GOD WE TRUST were moved to new positions. At the same time the Mint altered the portrait of Washington by adding little curlicue-and-squiggle hair details.

THE PROGRAM IN OPERATION

The first coin in the series, from Delaware reverse, was produced in 1999. It was followed in order with the coins of Pennsylvania, New Jersey, Georgia, and Connecticut. The public reception was excellent, and numismatists were pleased as well. For this and other quarters as they were develop, hobby newspapers *Coin World* and *Numismatic News* have carried week-by-week coverage, beginning with early design ideas and concepts, through sketches, continuing to the approved motifs, coinage, and distribution.

Selecting a design to truly represent a state has not always been easy or problem-free. Controversies have erupted, not only with the motifs chosen, but sometimes afterward when the artist found that the design approved was vastly altered by the Mint staff. In practice, it is the Mint that has made most of the final decisions—and not each state's advisory committees. In particular, there was

a big brouhaha with the 2003 Missouri motif, for which the Mint changed the artist's work dramatically.

ARTISTIC INFUSION

In 2004, the United States Mint implemented the novel Artistic Infusion Program, an effort to bring the talents of private-sector artists under the wing of the government. Eighteen "master designers" and six "associate designers" would create motifs for American coins and medals. An orientation meeting was held at the Philadelphia Mint in February of the same year. "Together, we will invigorate the artistry of coin design in America," Mint Director Henrietta Holsman Fore announced.

DIVERSITY IN DESIGNS

If anything, the designs have been diverse. No two have been alike, although some share similarities (the Wright brothers' biplane flies across both the North Carolina and Ohio coins, for example, and American bison inhabit more than one design). Some states have opted for a somewhat bland treatment of political geography—showing an outline of the state boundaries—but many have risen to the occasion with more interesting designs showing a panoply of themes.

KEY TO COLLECTING STATE QUARTERS

In all instances, for both copper-nickel clad and 90% silver state quarters, circulation-strike mintages have run into the hundreds of millions and Proofs in the high hundreds of thousands. Accordingly, the four varieties of each issue were readily available in the year they were minted, and after that time the market supply has been generous.

There have been no lack of comments from present-day numismatists concerning their likes and dislikes among the state quarters. Of course, anyone can make their own list of favorites. No doubt if 1,000 collectors were surveyed, no two commentaries would be alike. Many choose to collect one of each design; or one from each Mint for each state (two per state per year), plus Proofs; or simply those that appeal to them. The key, perhaps, is simply to have fun—a theme that applies to much of numismatics.

THE FUTURE OF THE STATE QUARTER PROGRAM

From the very start of the program some have suggested that the "States of the Union" concept be extended to include the District of Columbia and certain territories and possessions. This comment by David L. Ganz appeared under the title "Senate Seeks Quarter Extension," in *Numismatic News*, August 3, 2004 (excerpt):

> Hopes that Congress will extend the state quarter program with an 11th year that will include Washington, D.C., and five insular territories took a boost July 8 when Sen. Bill Nelson, D-Fla., introduced S. 2626, a bill to provide for a circulating quarter dollar coin program to honor the District of Columbia, the Commonwealth of Puerto Rico, Guam, American Samoa, the United States Virgin Islands, and the Commonwealth of the Northern Mariana Islands.

We will all have to stay tuned to watch developments. In the meantime, we can enjoy an exciting, rarely disappointing, often controversial, and always interesting coin series.

1999 ' DELAWARE

The first coin out of the gate, so to speak, was widely appreciated by collectors. Depicted is Caesar Rodney on horseback, on an 80-mile ride to Philadelphia, then the seat of the Continental Congress. On July 1, 1776, despite severe discomfort and illness, as a delegate from the colony of Delaware he cast the deciding vote that called for independence from England. History records his many accomplishments, including as a signer of the Declaration of Independence, a soldier, and holder of many offices in the state.

Citizens of the state were invited to send ideas for the design to the Delaware Arts Council, resulting in more than 300 entries. Certain of these were sent to the Mint, where they were converted into drawings. Three concepts were selected, these being Caesar Rodney, an allegorical Miss Liberty, and a quill-and-pen design. The office of

Governor Thomas R. Carper conducted a limited email and telephone poll, garnering 1,519 votes, of which 948 were for Rodney, 235 for Miss Liberty, and 336 for the writing materials.

The designer of the winning motif was Eddy Seger, not credited on the coin, per Mint policy. "There needs to be recognition given where it's due," Seger was quoted as saying later (in the *Columbia Missourian*, November 17, 2002). "Things are being turned around. It really is about states, not the United States Mint." It seems that Seger's design was closest to the final motif, but his horse was riding in the opposite direction. There is no known portrait of Caesar Rodney, so one artist's guess was as good as another's from the standpoint of history. This situation was hardly new, for when the 1892 World's Columbian Exposition commemorative half dollar was designed, it was a puzzle as to which of many different versions of Christopher Columbus should be chosen, none of which was proved to be an authentic portrait.

This bold yet simple design, with the horse and rider quickly catching the eye, is in my opinion one of the best in the entire series.

This coin portrait of Christopher Columbus, like the depiction of Caesar Rodney on the Delaware quarter, is more of a guess than an exact likeness.

FACTS AND FIGURES

Reverse design: Rider on horseback headed to the left, with CAESAR RODNEY near the left border. At the upper right is THE FIRST STATE, signifying Delaware's position. Other features are standard.

Reverse designed by: Eddy Seger, an art and drama teacher, per information given by the Public Information Office of the United States Mint in early 1999. However, after reading about this in *Coin World*, February 15, 1999, certain officials from the state of Delaware stated that no single person deserved the credit, and at least six different sketches depicted the equestrian Rodney theme.

Reverse die created by Mint sculptor-engraver: William Cousins

Engraver's initials and location: WC conjoined, with the top of the C missing on some impressions due to over-polishing of the die, giving an appearance of "UL." The initials are located to the left, between the horse's extended hoof and the border.

Statehood date (ratification of the U.S. Constitution): December 7, 1787

Official coin release date: January 4, 1999

Circulation strike mintage (clad composition) • 1999-P Delaware: 373,400,000; **1999-D Delaware:** 401,424,000 • The Mint offered various purchase options to collectors, including quantities in Mint-sewn cloth bags, a program that would be continued with later issues.

Proof mintage (clad composition) • 1999-S Delaware: 3,713,359

Proof mintage (silver composition) • 1999-S Delaware: 800,000

1999 · PENNSYLVANIA

The design of the 1999 Pennsylvania quarter is a small collage of items relating to the state. The design, an outline map, includes a representation of the 14-foot statue from the top of the State Capitol building, a keystone, and a motto. The statue itself was relatively unknown prior to its appearance here, and probably not one in a thousand residents of the state could have identified it as *Commonwealth*, by a New York sculptor. "Her right arm extends in kindness, and her left arm grasps a ribbon mace to symbolize justice," a Mint news release noted, although I am not quite sure what a "ribbon mace" is.

This was selected from one of five final designs, from more than 5,300 ideas submitted. These were reviewed by the Commemorative Quarter Committee, which included Donald Carlucci, president of the Pennsylvania Association of Numismatists. Also aboard was Dr. Brent Glass, who a few years later was named as director of the Smithsonian Institution. Four of these motifs passed muster with committees, after which Governor Tom Ridge made the final choice. Then at the Mint the models and dies were produced.

This 1876 depiction of Pennsylvania's emblem emphasizes the state's position as the "keystone" of the old colonies.

FACTS AND FIGURES

Reverse design: At the center is an outline map of the state, with the goddess *Commonwealth* prominent at the center, holding a standard topped by an eagle. She is elegantly styled, seems to have a bouffant hairdo, and would serve well as a large motif on any coin (to the author, a return to the classics, a la the dime, quarter, and half dollar of 1916, would be welcome). At the upper left of the map is a keystone in pebbled bas-relief, reflecting "the Keystone State," a motto used on license plates and elsewhere—and reflective of Pennsylvania's position near the center of the original 13 colonies, although a Mint release suggests, "the modern persistence of this designation is justified in view of the key position of Pennsylvania in the economic, social, and political development of the United States." To the right on the map is a more formal motto, VIRTUE / LIBERTY / INDEPENDENCE, in three lines.

Reverse designed by: Roland Hinton Perry is deserving of some small part of the credit. The design is a composite motif highlighted by *Commonwealth*, an allegorical goddess created by Perry, a New York sculptor, and placed on the State Capitol dome in Harrisburg on May 25, 1905. The construction of the Capitol erupted into a great scandal, a *cause célèbre*, as corrupt politicians accepted huge sums from contractors.

Die created by Mint sculptor-engraver: John Mercanti

Engraver's initials and location: JM. Immediately below the bottom border of the state (a.k.a. the Mason-Dixon Line) and to the right of the goddess' leg.

Statehood date (ratification of the U.S. Constitution): December 12, 1787

Official coin release date: March 8, 1999

Circulation strike mintage (clad composition) • **1999-P Pennsylvania:** 349,000,000 • **1999-D Pennsylvania:** 358,332,000

Proof mintage (clad composition) • **1999-S Pennsylvania:** 3,713,359

Proof mintage (silver composition) • **1999-S Pennsylvania:** 800,000

1999 ' NEW JERSEY

The 1999 New Jersey quarter furnished the first truly familiar motif on a state coin, this of the well-known scene taken from the 1851 painting by Emmanuel Leutze, *Washington Crossing the Delaware*, also used in 1976 for 13¢ stamps in connection with the Bicentennial. Accordingly, it may be proper to credit Leutze as the designer of the coin. The topic commemorates a daring exploit on Christmas night, 1776, when General Washington and troops of the Continental Army rowed across the ice-strewn water, landed in Trenton on the New Jersey side, and surprised the British enemy, taking more than 900 prisoners in the process. Times were difficult for the American soldiers, and this accomplishment, quickly followed by a victory at Princeton, did much to lift morale.

Once again, a committee of citizens was appointed to review ideas for the quarter design, finally selecting five. Governor Christine Todd Whitman made the final selection in cooperation with the Fine Arts Commission.

This coin is one of just a handful of coins to feature the same person on each side—others being in the commemorative series, including the 1900 Lafayette dollar (General Lafayette), the 1921 Missouri half dollar (Daniel Boone), and the 1936 Elgin half dollar (a pioneer). So far the 1990 Eisenhower dollar is the only legal tender coin to depict the same person twice *on the same side*, but who knows what the state quarter program will bring in the future?

Like George Washington, who appears twice on the New Jersey quarter, French General Lafayette occupies both the front and back of this 1900 commemorative dollar.

90 years later, Dwight Eisenhower would appear twice on this silver dollar—but both times on the front!

FACTS AND FIGURES

Reverse design: Washington and accompanying soldiers in a rowboat crossing the Delaware River from Pennsylvania to New Jersey, adapted from a painting created by Emmanuel Leutze. A soldier is seated on the prow and is pushing an ice floe with his foot. The Father of Our Country and at least one other person are standing in the vessel, seemingly a rather risky thing to do in the dark on a river filled with drifting ice. Moreover, Washington's foot is blocking an oarlock that could be used effectively by the paddler in the bow, who is forced to do without one. Below is the two-line inscription, CROSSROADS OF THE REVOLUTION. Other features are standard.

Reverse designed by: Adapted from a painting created by Emmanuel Leutze.

Die created by Mint sculptor-engraver: Alfred F. Maletsky

Engraver's initials and location: AM. Between the end of the boat and the rim on the right. The initials are tiny.

Statehood date (ratification of the U.S. Constitution): December 18, 1787

Official coin release date: May 17, 1999

Circulation strike mintage (clad composition) • 1999-P New Jersey: 363,200,000 • **1999-D New Jersey:** 299,028,000

Proof mintage (clad composition) • 1999-S New Jersey: 3,713,359

Proof mintage (silver composition) • 1999-S New Jersey: 800,000

1999 · GEORGIA

On the 1999 Georgia quarter we see a montage of topics relating to the state, similar in concept to the Pennsylvania issue. An outline map has at the center a peach, the best-known symbol of that southern district. The official state tree, the live oak, is remembered by branches there from—one on each side. On a flowing ribbon is the motto, WISDOM JUSTICE MODERATION, seemingly good precepts for anyone to observe.

The Georgia Council for the Arts was enlisted by Governor Zell Miller to receive and develop motifs. Eventually five finalists were chosen, then further narrowed to four, with the winner being picked by the governor.

The U.S. Mint describes the Peach State's motif:

Just from studying the Georgia quarter design, one can learn a lot about the fourth state of the Union. The selected design prominently features the peach—a symbol long associated with the state—within the confines of a silhouetted outline of the state. Live Oak sprigs border the central design paying homage to the official state tree, the Live Oak. And if you ever need to know the Georgia state motto, simply look across the top of the design, where the words "Wisdom, Justice, Moderation," grace a hanging banner.

James Oglethorpe was the wealthy English soldier and philanthropist who colonized what became the state of Georgia. He secured a charter for the colony in 1732; his idea was to begin a refuge for unemployed debtors freshly released from prison.

FACTS AND FIGURES

Reverse design: An outline map of Georgia with a peach at the center, with a leaf attached to a stem. To the left and right are branches of live oak. A loosely arranged ribbon bears the motto WISDOM JUSTICE MODERATION in three sections. Other features are standard.

Reverse designed by: Identity not publicized.

Die created by Mint sculptor-engraver: T. James Ferrell

Engraver's initials and location: TJF in italic capitals. Below the lower side of the branch stem on the right.

Statehood date (ratification of the U.S. Constitution): January 2, 1788

Official coin release date: July 19, 1999

Circulation strike mintage (clad composition) • **1999-P Georgia:** 451,188,000 • **1999-D Georgia:** 488,744,000

Proof mintage (clad composition) • **1999-S Georgia:** 3,713,359

Proof mintage (silver composition) • **1999-S Georgia:** 800,000

1999 · CONNECTICUT

A numismatist could make a specialty, or at least a side activity, in assembling a collection of coins, tokens, medals, and paper money featuring the Charter Oak—to which the 1999 Connecticut quarter would be the latest addition. Those who follow commemoratives know of the 1935 Connecticut Tercentenary half dollar with this motif, while for others a bill from the Charter Oak Bank of Hartford, chartered by the state on August 22, 1853, would be a dandy acquisition—except that 90% of those on the market are contemporary counterfeits, not the real thing. Such currency, as well as coins and medals, feature the state's best-known tree, dear for a recess within its trunk in which early colonists secreted their royal charter when agents of King James II desired to confiscate it. In 1855, Charles Dewolf Brownell created a painting of the tree from life, an image used on the 1935 Connecticut Tercentenary half dollar, a commemorative stamp, and elsewhere.

This 1935 half dollar commemorates the 300th anniversary of the founding of Connecticut as a colony. It shows the famous Charter Oak.

Governor John G. Rowland set up the Connecticut Coin Design Competition, which attracted somewhat more than a hundred entries, 19 of which showed the Charter Oak. Apparently, five were selected from these 19, sent off to the Mint, reviewed, and reviewed again, after which one was picked. The winning tree certainly does not show *the* Charter Oak—one of the biggest goofs on any American coin with a stated historical motif.

It is too bad that some other Connecticut-related motif wasn't used—such as Jumbo the elephant (owner P.T. Barnum lived in the state), the Bienecke Library at Yale, a Colt revolver (made in Hartford) as part of a Wells-Fargo stagecoach scene, a sailing ship from the Mystic Seaport Museum, or the façade on the old penny arcade at Savin Rock Park.

P.T. Barnum is honored on another Connecticut commemorative: the half dollar of 1935.

FACTS AND FIGURES

Reverse design: A rather bushy-appearing tree, in no way resembling the Charter Oak, with a small trunk, and leafless (presumably from the frost of winter. Above the ground at the lower left is THE CHARTER OAK. Other features are standard.

Reverse designed by: Identity not publicized. However, Randy Jones is credited by the Independent Grading Service (IGS) as the designer.

Die created by Mint sculptor-engraver: T. James Ferrell

Engraver's initials and location: TJF in italic capitals. On the border to the right of M (UNUM).

Statehood date (ratification of the U.S. Constitution): January 9, 1788

Official coin release date: October 12, 1999

Circulation strike mintage (clad composition) • 1999-P Connecticut: 688,744,000 • **1999-D Connecticut:** 657,880,000

Proof mintage (clad composition) • 1999-S Connecticut: 3,713,359

Proof mintage (silver composition) • 1999-S Connecticut: 800,000

2000 · MASSACHUSETTS

In February 1998, Governor Paul Cellucci began the process leading to the creation of a suitable design, after which more than 100 youngsters provided sketches. Ten members on an advisory council narrowed the entries down to five. In June 1999, Governor Cellucci and Lt. Governor Jane Swift announced the winning design.

If you have a 1925 Lexington-Concord commemorative half dollar depicting Daniel Chester French's *Minuteman* statue on the obverse, then you'll recognize the same motif on the back side of the 2000 Massachusetts quarter. The statue itself stands not far from the "rude bridge that arched the flood," evocative of the early days of the American Revolution. On the new coin the statue is shown with a textured outline map of THE BAY STATE (per the legend), complete with such details as Nantucket and Martha's Vineyard islands (among others) and a star indicating the location of Boston.

Considering that the same motif had been used on a commemorative coin, postage as well as savings stamps, and elsewhere, to set up a 10-member advisory council and engage in other hoopla turned out to be a wasted effort. Well, perhaps it was not, for two fifth-grade students had the same idea and shared the recognition, including being featured guests at the official launch ceremony—a heartwarming situation for them and their classmates, all of whom were invited to be on hand at the event in Boston's historic Faneuil Hall.

Daniel Chester French's *Minuteman* is seen on another coin, this one a commemorative half dollar from 1925.

FACTS AND FIGURES

Reverse design: Outline map of Massachusetts (stippled background of uniform height, not representing topological elevations) with French's *Minuteman* statue superimposed. The location of Boston is noted by a raised five-pointed star. At the right, offshore in the ocean, is the three line inscription, THE BAY STATE. Other features are standard.

Reverse designed by: Two fifth-grade schoolchildren illustrating the famous *Minuteman* statue by Daniel Chester French.

Die created by Mint sculptor-engraver: Thomas D. Rogers (who in life, but not on the coin, usually styles himself as Thomas D. Rogers, Sr.)

Engraver's initials and location: TDR. Below the bottom left side of the map.

Statehood date (ratification of the U.S. Constitution): February 6, 1788

Official coin release date: January 3, 2000 • There were two launch ceremonies, the first such instance in the state quarter program. One was held at Faneuil Hall in Boston. The other was at the Philadelphia Mint, with a "first coin," so to speak, being struck by remote contact when Governor Paul Cellucci, Mint Director Philip Diehl, Mint engraver Thomas D. Rogers, and the two schoolchildren (by that time in the seventh grade at the Belmont Day School and the sixth grade at St. Bernard's Elementary School) who created the original design, combined to push a button at the Faneuil Hall event. Then Director Diehl held up a coin to show the *Boston* audience, citing the miracles of modern technology.

Circulation strike mintage (clad composition) • **2000-P Massachusetts:** 628,600,000 • **2000-D Massachusetts:** 535,184,000

Proof mintage (clad composition) • **2000-S Massachusetts:** 4,020,083

Proof mintage (silver composition) • **2000-S Massachusetts:** 856,400

2000 ⟩ MARYLAND

In the opinion of many collectors, Maryland (THE OLD LINE STATE, as proclaimed on the coins) laid an egg with the design of this quarter dollar. Featuring the top part of the State House, called a "striking dome" in Mint literature, this supposedly wonderful subject that used up Maryland's once-in-a-lifetime coin opportunity is also "the country's largest wooden dome built without nails." And, in case you wonder, the quoted motto is in honor of its "troops of the line," this also from Mint text. In addition, there are two branches from a white oak (the state tree), complete with a few acorns (but no squirrels).

A Mint news release gave these details of the release:

> Annapolis, March 13, 2000: In the Maryland State House Governor's Conference Room—an upstairs chamber decorated with portraits from Maryland's past—Governor Parris N. Glendening added a new contribution to the Old Line State's history. Before a group of onlookers, he unveiled the official Maryland state quarter in the very building the new coin honors....

The motto OLD LINE STATE, less familiar than Maryland's nickname of The Free State, was started by George Washington in 1776. *Washington Post* writer Lori Montgomery discussed the name in a March 14, 2000 article:

> It seems Washington himself bestowed the nickname on Maryland after the Battle of Long Island in August 1776, when a line of Maryland troops held off the British while Washington retreated. Thousands died, and many Maryland soldiers were buried in Brooklyn, said Maryland state archivist Edward C.

Papenfuse. Thereafter, Washington referred to Maryland troops as "the old line—meaning they were always there, reliable, Papenfuse said....

Historians and other observers might wonder, what else (other than the obscure State House dome) might have been featured on this coin? How about the *original* Washington Monument in Mount Vernon Square. Or an oyster or a crab. Or a Baltimore clipper, a ship famous in its time. Or a locomotive and string of cars on the Baltimore & Ohio Railroad. Or the Star Spangled Banner (Fort McHenry was in Baltimore)...

The Latin motto shown on this seal, *Crescite et Multiplicamini*, means "Increase and Multiply."

FACTS AND FIGURES

Reverse design: Wooden dome and supporting structure on the Maryland State House in Annapolis, with THE OLD LINE STATE in two lines, and with branches of white oak to each side. Other features are standard.

Reverse designed by: Bill Krawczewicz

Die created by Mint sculptor-engraver: Thomas D. Rogers

Engraver's initials and location: TDR. Below an acorn and above M (in UNUM).

Statehood date (ratification of the U.S. Constitution): April 28, 1788

Official coin release date: March 13, 2000

Circulation strike mintage (clad composition) • **2000-P Maryland:** 678,200,000 • **2000-D Maryland:** 556,532,000

Proof mintage (clad composition) • **2000-S Maryland:** 4,020,083

Proof mintage (silver composition) • **2000-S Maryland:** 856,400

2000 · SOUTH CAROLINA

The South Carolina Numismatic Society had a hand in picking this design. The motif is the most natural (botany and zoology type of natural) seen to date in the series, what with a palmetto tree, a Carolina wren, and some yellow jessamine flowers. These motifs, and the motto, THE PALMETTO STATE, are on and around an outline map of South Carolina.

Various committees were involved in searching for and devising designs. The choice narrowed to just three. Then, according to the U.S. Mint's literature:

> Governor Jim Hodges then made his final decision, indicating that the palmetto tree represents South Carolina's strength; the Carolina wren's song symbolizes the hospitality of the state's people; and the yellow jessamine, a delicate golden

bloom—a sign of coming spring—is part of South Carolina's vast natural beauty.

The launching ceremony, May 24, 2000, was described in this *Numismatic News* account (June 13, 2000):

> Jay Johnson was confirmed as Mint director by vote of the U.S. Senate May 24. He was sworn in by Treasury Secretary Lawrence H. Summers, May 25 and on May 26 he was in Columbia, S.C., for the ceremonial debut of the South Carolina quarter.
>
> U.S. Treasurer Mary Ellen Withrow and Johnson helped South Carolina governor Jim Hodges launch the coin at ceremonies at Dutch Fork Elementary School.
>
> To start the event, Hodges presented the new quarter to students. Attributing the success of the coin

program to the youth of the nation, Withrow said, "Many of the ideas for the South Carolina quarter design came from elementary students who are enthusiastic about our nation's culture and history." For Johnson, it was his first public appearance in his new job. He had been sworn in just the day before.

An earlier U.S. coin—the 1936 half dollar commemorating the 150th anniversary of Columbia, South Carolina—also featured a palmetto tree.

FACTS AND FIGURES

Reverse design: Outline map of South Carolina with Carolina wren and yellow jessamine flowers to the left; a palmetto, with severed trunk, is shown to the right. THE PALMETTO STATE in three lines at the upper left. The position of Columbia, the state capital, is indicated by a raised five-pointed star. Other features are standard.

Reverse designed by: Identity not publicized.

Die created by Mint sculptor-engraver: Thomas D. Rogers

Engraver's initials and location: TDR. Below the right side of the palmetto ground.

Statehood date (ratification of the U.S. Constitution): May 23, 1788

Official coin release date: May 22, 2000

Circulation strike mintage (clad composition) • 2000-P South Carolina: 742,576,000 • **2000-D South Carolina:** 566,208,000. Not included in this figure are these novel coins: at the Denver Mint a die "bearing a South Carolina quarter dollar reverse that was intentionally paired with a 2001-D Sacagawea dollar obverse to strike a mule on a manganese-brass clad dollar planchet," a caper that was detected. However, "it is not known whether specimens ...escaped the mint facilities. None have been reported in the coin market" (from *Coin World*, November 3, 2003).

Proof mintage (clad composition) • 2000-S South Carolina: 402,008

Proof mintage (silver composition) • 2000-S South Carolina: 856,400

2000 · NEW HAMPSHIRE

As a resident of the Granite State, this quarter is one of my favorites. I was responsible, in a way, for the final design, although I did not create it. By the way, of all state motifs this is one of those most criticized by others—people from out-of-state just don't understand why we like the thing!

Ideas for depictions on the quarter were aplenty. Finally, the choice narrowed down to just two: 1. A wooden spire-topped "meetinghouse" of the type said to have been a forum for town meetings generations ago, and, in many New Hampshire communities, still used today. 2. A covered bridge crossing a stream.

These sketches were sent to Philadelphia, where the ideas were reviewed at the Mint. Committee member Kenneth Bressett, long-time friend of mine and editor of the best-selling *Guide Book of United States Coins*, sent me copies of several variations of these two final contenders.

I was rather disappointed. To me, the meetinghouse with four spires resembled a standard design for a Baptist church of the old days, not a nonsectarian town hall. As to the covered bridge, while there are dozens in the state, they do not immediately pop to mind as emblematic of the place. I mentioned these concerns, then suggested to Ken: "Why not use the Old Man of the Mountain?"

This referred to the Great Stone Face, as it is (or was) sometimes called—a 40-foot rocky outcrop on Cannon Mountain in Franconia Notch that has been the symbol of the state for a long time. It even attracted the attention of Daniel Webster, who penned a commentary reproduced on a large sign nearby. Ken said that the idea had been considered but the Mint had stated that the motif was too heavy on one side, not balanced. I found this curious, as for years the New Hampshire State Turnpike Commission had been using tokens with the Old Man of the Mountain on them—well struck and durable. I sent some of these to Ken, he saw that coining was practical, and soon the Old Man was adopted.

At the launching ceremony on August 7, 2000, scheduled to be held in the State House but moved at the last minute to a large room in the nearby New Hampshire Historical Society, I covered the event for *Coin World*.

Unfortunately, on May 3, 2003, the rocky outcrop crumbled to rubble, the victim of thousands of years of weathering—warm summers alternating with icy winters. The Old Man was no more, giving the coin the unwanted distinction of being the first state reverse quarter that depicted something in existence when the coin was struck, but now, in effect, a *commemorative* of times past, but not forgotten.

FACTS AND FIGURES

Reverse design: The Old Man of the Mountain, on the right side of the coin, extending to the center, gazing upon a field in which the state motto, LIVE FREE OR DIE, lies. Nine stars, representing the state's order of ratifying the Constitution, are at the left border.

Reverse designed by: Unknown, one of many traditional versions of the famous icon used in many places, including on a commemorative stamp. Adapted from a quarter-size brass token used on routes I-93 and I-95 in the state (this comment for collectors who like trivia).

Die created by Mint sculptor-engraver: William Cousins

Engraver's initials and location: WC. Below the Old Man of the Mountain and above M (in UNUM).

Statehood date (ratification of the U.S. Constitution): June 21, 1788

Official coin release date: August 7, 2000 • The ceremony was held in Concord at the New Hampshire Historical Society, a location rescheduled at the last minute from the nearby State House. Governor Jean Shaheen was on hand. Representing the Mint was David Pickens, with Mary Ellen Withrow, treasurer of the United States.

Circulation strike mintage (clad composition) • **2000-P New Hampshire:** 673,040,000 • **2000-D New Hampshire:** 495,976,000

Proof mintage (clad composition) • **2000-S New Hampshire:** 4,020,083

Proof mintage (silver composition) • **2000-S New Hampshire:** 856,400

2000 ⟩ VIRGINIA

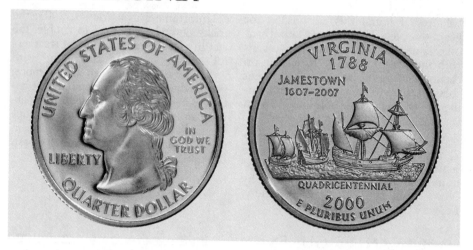

A pleasing little flotilla of boats— the *Susan Constant, Godspeed,* and *Discovery*—graces the center of the 2000 Virginia quarter. The boats carry brave emigrants on their way to what would become Jamestown, the first permanent English settlement in the New World. Under a charter granted to the Virginia Company by King James on April 10, 1606, the vessels left London on September 20 of the same year. On May 12, 1607, the group of 104 men and boys landed on an island in the James River about 60 miles into the Chesapeake Bay from the ocean. This was 13 years prior to the better-known arrival of the Pilgrims at Massachusetts, far to the north. The Virginia quarter bears legends relating to the 400th anniversary of the event (an observance somewhat premature, but there were no complaints).

Decades earlier, celebrating the *300th* anniversary, right on target, the Jamestown Exposition was held in Virginia. The indefatigable coin dealer Farran Zerbe set up an exhibit and sold souvenirs. An effort was made to authorize commemorative coins, but as recent issues such as the 1903 Louisiana Purchase Exposition and the 1904 and 1905 Lewis and Clark gold dollars had each fallen far short of their anticipated sales, there was no interest in Congress for creating more of the same.

To choose a design for the 2000 Virginia quarter, Susan F. Dewey, state treasurer, was appointed as the liaison person with the United States Mint. Several different state agencies and offices as well as many citizens joined the effort, ultimately creating thousands of responses. Governor James Gilmore III made the final selection and the Treasury Department nodded its approval.

In 1936, a commemorative half dollar was struck to honor the 150th year of the charter of the city of Lynchburg, Virginia. The obverse features a portrait of Senator Carter Glass. The reverse shows Liberty standing, with the old Lynchburg courthouse in the background.

Another 1936 commemorative half dollar honored the bicentennial of Norfolk, Virginia's growth from a township to a royal borough (and the 300th anniversary of its original land grant). It features the City Seal of Norfolk and the city's Royal Mace.

FACTS AND FIGURES

Reverse design: Three ships under sail en route to a destination that would become known as Jamestown. At the upper left is the inscription, JAMESTOWN 1607-2007, and beneath the seascape is the word QUADRI-CENTENNIAL. Other features are standard.

Reverse designed by: Paris Ashton, a graphic artist, was credited by the Independent Grading Service (IGS) as the designer.

Die created by Mint sculptor-engraver: Edgar Z. Steever

Engraver's initials and location: EZS. On the surface of the ocean at the lower right corner of that feature.

Statehood date (ratification of the U.S. Constitution): June 25, 1788

Official coin release date: October 16, 2000

Circulation strike mintage (clad composition) • **2000-P Virginia:** 943,000,000 (record high to this point) • **2000-D Virginia:** 651,616,000

Proof mintage (clad composition) • **2000-S Virginia:** 4,020,083

Proof mintage (silver composition) • **2000-S Virginia:** 856,400

2001 · NEW YORK

The New York state quarter of 2001 continued the map concept used for the 1999 Pennsylvania and Georgia coins and the 2000 issues of Massachusetts and South Carolina. The New York design showed some details, including lines added to reflect the course of a waterway using part of the Hudson River and all of the Erie Canal. The Statue of Liberty, officially known as *Liberty Enlightening the World*, is on the left side, nicely balancing the heavier map area to the right. The statue is a popular collector subject, used on 1986 commemorative coins and nearly 30 different varieties of postage stamps.

In keeping with procedures used elsewhere, the governor of the state called for designs from the public, attracting many entries. Finally, five motifs were chosen, these being the aforementioned statue as well as Henry Hudson and his *Half Moon* ship, a scene depicted on the historical *Battle of Saratoga* painting, and the Federal Building on Wall Street, New York City.

Citizens were invited to contact the governor's office to vote for their favorite. The winner, garnering an impressive 76% of responses, is described below, this from details provided by the United States Mint:

> The New York design celebrates the "Empire State" as a point of entry for millions of immigrants seeking the political freedom and democracy that American citizenship provides. President Grover Cleveland accepted the Statue of Liberty, a gift from the people of France, on behalf of the United States on October 28, 1886. Lady Liberty was designated a National Monument on October 15, 1924 and underwent extensive restoration for her remarkable centennial on July 4, 1986. Governor George E. Pataki asked the

United States Mint to add the line tracing the Hudson River and the route of the Erie Canal because of the vital developmental role of the waterways.

The new quarters were released in January 2001. As it turned out, the attacks on the twin towers of the World Trade Center on September 11 of the same year took attention away from just about everything else, and rightly so. No doubt if a design had been picked after that time, the World Trade Center would have received consideration.

FACTS AND FIGURES

Reverse design: A textured map of New York State (with apparent topological relief, but not to scale), with a recessed line showing the Hudson River and Erie Canal waterway (at the same-level, with no locks in the Erie Canal). The river is shown only to the point at which it joins the canal. The Statue of Liberty is to the left and the inscription, GATEWAY TO FREEDOM is to the right, not a replacement from the time honored EXCELSIOR motto, or even THE EMPIRE STATE, but, seemingly a comment on New York City harbor, home of the statue, being an entry port for those emigrating from distant lands. Eleven stars are added at the upper left and right borders, past NEW YORK, nicely adding to the design and representing the order in which the state ratified the Constitution, this being the second quarter design to show this progression (New Hampshire was the first).

Reverse designed by: Daniel Carr. *Liberty Enlightening the World* was designed by French sculptor Frédéric Auguste Bartholdi, and thus he should get some peripheral credit or at least a slight nod (as with Daniel Chester French for the Massachusetts quarter).

Die created by Mint sculptor-engraver: Alfred F. Maletsky

Engraver's initials and location: AM in italic capitals below the left border of the map.

Statehood date (ratification of the U.S. Constitution): July 26, 1788

Official coin release date: January 2, 2001, for general circulation. • On January 8, 2001, the launch ceremony was held at the New York State Museum in Albany, in connection with the related "Gateway to Freedom" exhibit.

Circulation strike mintage (clad composition) • **2001-P New York:** 655,400,000 • **2001-D New York:** 619,640,000

Proof mintage (clad composition) • **2001-S New York:** 3,093,274

Proof mintage (silver composition) • **2001-S New York:** 889,697

2001 · NORTH CAROLINA

The 2001 North Carolina quarter depicts the Wright brothers' airplane that on December 17, 1903, flew a distance of 120 feet among the sand dunes of Kitty Hawk, on the seacoast of the state. Although S.P. Langley, backed by many assertions from the Smithsonian Institution, claimed that Langley was first in the manned flight of a heavier-than-air machine, most historians have credited the Wrights. Perhaps the matter will never be resolved to everyone's satisfaction—sort of like who was the first to reach the North Pole, Cook or Peary?

The image on the coin is loosely adapted from a contemporary photograph by John P. Daniels, now with the standing figure of Wilbur Wright larger in the foreground, as he observes the historic flight with brother Orville lying flat on his stomach at the controls. Concepts for the plane were developed and the craft constructed in Ohio, home of the Wright brothers, who operated a bicycle shop. Henry Ford, who collected all sorts of things, later bought the shop operated by the Wrights in Dayton, and moved it to Greenfield Village in Dearborn, Michigan, where it can be seen today. Later, in 2002, Ohio would also memorialize the Wright brothers.

Ideas for the coin design were solicited by the North Carolina Department of Cultural Resources, which set up the North Carolina Commemorative Coin Committee. The resultant publicity drew many submissions. Alternate motifs included the Wright biplane superimposed on an outline map of the state, and the Cape Hatteras lighthouse (also on a map, and the same seashore prominence, but with a sand dune and seagulls). As Okracoke Inlet, nearby, is famous for its supposed buried treasure, it might have been interesting to add a chest of doubloons! On June 5, 2000, the Committee and Governor James B. Hunt picked the "First Flight" motif, as it was called. The FIRST FLIGHT inscription, eventually appearing on the coin, caused some confusion as a slightly different version, FIRST IN FLIGHT, had been used on state license plates since 1981.

North Carolina's state emblem illustrates an abundance of agriculture and industry, with a maiden holding a Phrygian cap representing liberty.

FACTS AND FIGURES

Reverse design: The first manned flight at Kitty Hawk, North Carolina, as taken from a famous photograph. The Wright biplane, flying toward the right, has Orville lying on his stomach, operating the controls. Above is FIRST FLIGHT. In the foreground are a bench and the large standing figure of Wilbur Wright (much larger than on the original photograph). Other features are standard.

Reverse designed by: Mary Ellen Robinson, "who submitted a drawing based upon the famous photograph," was credited by the Independent Grading Service (IGS) as the designer (*Coin World*, September 17, 2001). Others credited posthumously the 1903 photographer, John P. Daniels.

Die created by Mint sculptor-engraver: John Mercanti

Engraver's initials and location: JM. Above the far right side of the ground.

Statehood date (ratification of the U.S. Constitution): November 21, 1789

Official coin release date: March 12, 2001

Circulation strike mintage (clad composition) • 2001-P North Carolina: 627,600,000 • **2001-D North Carolina:** 427,876,000.

Proof mintage (clad composition) • 2001-S North Carolina: 3,093,274

Proof mintage (silver composition) • 2001-S North Carolina: 889,697

2001 · RHODE ISLAND

The Rhode Island quarter of 2001 is inscribed as the OCEAN STATE, reflecting the importance of the sea, including Narragansett Bay, a vast inlet of the Atlantic. The motif illustrates a vintage sailboat gliding across the waves before the wind, evocative of the America's Cup races centered there for more than a half century. In the distance is the Pell Bridge.

Governor Lincoln Almond authorized the Rhode Island State Council on the Arts to set up the Coin Concept Advisory Panel. Citizens of the state were invited to submit ideas, and more than 500 were received. The choice was narrowed down to three designs, after which it was open voting via libraries, the State House, and the Internet. Of the 34,566 votes cast, 57% were for the sailboat design. The Mint hired Thomas Carr, a Colorado artist responsible for the 2001 New York quarter, to create the motif used on the coin, an effort that most numismatists considered to be a great success.

The state emblem of Rhode Island features a strong maritime connection.

This Rhode Island medal of the Revolutionary War era was struck in 1778 or 1779. It shows the flagship of British Admiral Howe at anchor off Conanicut Island (near Newport). The reverse shows the retreat of American forces in 1778, pursued by Howe's forces. (The next year the tables were turned, and Howe and his ships had to retreat.) This was a piece of political propaganda, probably struck in England, aimed at persuading the Dutch not to sign the Treaty of Armed Neutrality.

FACTS AND FIGURES

Reverse design: A sailboat heading to the left before the wind. Deck details are visible, but no people are obvious. In the distance is the Pell Bridge, of the suspension type, with THE OCEAN STATE above. Other features are standard.

Reverse designed by: Daniel Carr. The boat was modeled after the *Reliance*, the 1903 winner of the America's Cup, a craft built in Bristol, Rhode Island, by the famous Herreshoff Manufacturing Co.

Die created by Mint sculptor-engraver: Thomas D. Rogers

Engraver's initials and location: TDR. At an angle on the surface of the waves at the lower right corner of this feature.

Statehood date (ratification of the U.S. Constitution): May 29, 1790

Official coin release date: May 21, 2001 • The launching ceremony was held at Fort Adams State Park in Newport, a facility in active use as a fort from 1824 to 1850. Governor Lincoln Almond and other state dignitaries were in attendance, including Mint Director Jay Johnson, plus an audience including students from the William J. Underwood Elementary School.

Circulation strike mintage (clad composition) • **2001-P Rhode Island:** 423,000,000 • **2001-D Rhode Island:** 447,100,000

Proof mintage (clad composition) • **2001-S Rhode Island:** 3,093,274

Proof mintage (silver composition) • **2001-S Rhode Island:** 889,697

2001 ˒ VERMONT

The 2001 Vermont quarter features a scene of two maple trees, not in the usual grove, but standing all by themselves, in early spring. Perhaps the grove is out of sight behind the observer. Maple sugaring is in progress, with sap buckets affixed to trees. Camel's Hump, the eponymous 4,083-foot landmark in the northern part of the Green Mountains range, forms the background.

Maple sugar production, earlier done by Native Americans, became an important industry in this state. The theme on the quarter offers a change from motifs earlier seen on Vermont-related coins, including the sun and forested ridge "landscape" design of the 1785 to 1786 copper pieces, and the Ira Allen/catamount design of the 1927 sesquicentennial commemorative half dollar.

Governor Howard Dean (later, in 2004, to achieve national attention for his aggressive but short-lived run for the Democratic presidential nomination) named the Vermont Arts Council to coordinate the quarter design. This group created five concepts, each including Camel's Hump, after which a casual survey was conducted by radio. Governor Dean made the final choice, based on artwork by Sarah-Lee Terrat, and sent it to the Treasury Department. The identity of Terrat was unknown to viewers of the coins, and only the initials of William Cousins, who altered the motif and made models, were featured.

This commemorative half dollar of 1927 honors Vermont's independence with a portrait of founder Ira Allen.

These Vermont "Landscape" coppers were struck in the 1780s, during the Revolutionary War. They would have served as currency during those troubled times.

FACTS AND FIGURES

Reverse design: Two maple trees, truncated at the top, standing alone, with an empty field or plain in the distance, beyond which is Camel's Hump, a prominence in the Green Mountain range. A standing man has his right hand at the top of one of four sap buckets in evidence. To the right is FREEDOM AND UNITY. Other features are standard.

Reverse designed by: Sarah-Lee Terrat

Die created by Mint sculptor-engraver: T. James Ferrell

Engraver's initials and location: TJF. In italic capitals above the ground at the far right.

Statehood date: March 4, 1791

Official coin release date: August 6, 2001 • A *Coin World* reader reported that he found a 2001-D Vermont quarter in circulation in St. Louis, Missouri, on April 1, 2001 (not an April Fool's joke). Some Kentucky quarters also left the starting gate early. The explanation seems to be that they strayed from quantities of these coins shipped to a separate location for packaging in 2001 Mint sets scheduled to be released at a much later date.

Circulation strike mintage (clad composition) • **2001-P Vermont:** 423,400,000 • **2001-D Vermont:** 459,404,000 • From August 6 to 9, 2001, the Mint had a special 72-hour sale event offering rolls, 100-coin bags, and 1,000-coin bags, resulting in 10,423,200 being sold to collectors and souvenir hunters.

Proof mintage (clad composition) • **2001-S Vermont:** 3,093,274

Proof mintage (silver composition) • **2001-S Vermont:** 889,697

2001 · KENTUCKY

The 2001 Kentucky quarter illustrates a hilltop mansion with a thoroughbred racehorse behind a fence in the foreground. The United States Mint described the design:

> Kentucky was the first state on the western frontier to join the Union and is one of four states to call itself a "commonwealth." Kentucky is home of the longest running annual horse race in the country, the Kentucky Derby.
>
> Also featured on the new quarter is another prominent symbol of Kentucky, Federal Hill, which has become known as My Old Kentucky Home. The design shows a side view of the famous Bardstown home where Stephen Foster wrote the state song, *My Old Kentucky Home.*

It may be of numismatic interest to mention that the portrait of Foster is depicted on the obverse of the 1936 Cincinnati commemorative half dollar. The composer wrote his memorable song at a cousin's home in 1818.

Governor Paul E. Hatton named his wife Judi to lead the Kentucky Quarter Project Committee. About 1,800 were received. These were narrowed to 12 final motifs, these being displayed in the Capitol building and shown on the Internet for people to review. The semi-finalists included designs of My Old Kentucky Home, America's First Frontier, a running thoroughbred, Daniel Boone with a long rifle, and similar themes.

The Kentucky coin caused a deterioration in the relationship between the U.S. Mint and design artists. Mint officials didn't look at the committee's sketches, asking instead for a description of the racehorse concept. The state then announced that Kentucky would

not officially recognize *any* individual designer, reasoning that the design (eventually engraved by Mint engraver Jim Ferrell) reflected many entries of similar appearance.

Stephen Foster, "America's Troubadour," who wrote *My Old Kentucky Home*, was shown on the 1936 Cincinnati Music Center half dollar.

FACTS AND FIGURES

Reverse design: The two-story Federal Hill house high on a rise, with 11 five-pointed stars erratically spaced on its sides. In the foreground a sleek and handsome horse stands behind a wooden fence. Above his head is "MY OLD KENTUCKY HOME" in quotation marks, thus indicating the inscription as a song title. Other features are standard.

Reverse designed by: Seemingly the design suggested by Ronald J. Inabit, although uncredited. The Independent Coin Grading Co. (ICG) signed a contract with contest entrant Benjamin Blair to sign "slabs" containing the coins, crediting him as the "concept artist."

Die created by Mint sculptor-engraver: T. James Ferrell

Engraver's initials and location: TJF. In italic capitals below the ground at the far right.

Statehood date: June 1, 1792

Official coin release date: October 15, 2001 • The launch ceremony was held on October 18th at the Federal Hill mansion shown on the coin, this being located in My Old Kentucky Home State Park in Bardstown. Mint Director Henrietta Holsman Fore, Governor Paul E. Patton, and others provided comments to the audience. First lady of the state, Judi Patton, who had been involved in the selection process, was unable to attend. • *Coin World* reported that 2001-D Kentucky quarters were found in circulation in Missouri on April 1 (by Matt Oser) and 6, joining an early-bird Vermont quarter also reported from the same state. The explanation seems to be that they strayed from quantities of these coins shipped to a separate location for packaging in 2001 mint sets scheduled to be released at a much later date.

Circulation strike mintage (clad composition) • **2001-P Kentucky:** 353,000,000 • **2001-D Kentucky:** 370,564,000

Proof mintage (clad composition) • **2001-S Kentucky:** 3,093,274

Proof mintage (silver composition) • **2001-S Kentucky:** 889,697

2002 · TENNESSEE

The motif of the 2002 Tennessee quarter is a course in musical history of the state. The web site of the U.S. Mint describes it thus:

> The design incorporates musical instruments and a score with the inscription "Musical Heritage." Three stars represent Tennessee's three regions, and the instruments symbolize each region's distinct musical style.
>
> The fiddle represents the Appalachian music of East Tennessee, the trumpet stands for the blues of West Tennessee for which Memphis is famous, and the guitar is for Central Tennessee, home to Nashville, the capital of country music.

Following the direction of the governor, a statewide contest for designs was launched in the spring of 2000, with the nearly 1,000 entries being evaluated by the seven members of the Tennessee Coin Commission. That group picked three favorite themes, including Musical Heritage, Ratification of the 19th Amendment, and Sequoyah (the creator of the Cherokee writing system).

On June 28, 2000, these were sent to the United States Mint. Nearly a year later, on June 26, 2001, the Mint sent five "approved renditions" of these ideas, from which Governor Donald Sundquist picked the one to be used.

The Tennessee quarter has a very "rare" guitar on it—one with six tuning pegs, but only *five* strings! Except that the five strings are regularly spaced, we might think that the sixth had been broken (perhaps during a musical gyration by Elvis Presley?). The trumpets on both the 2002 Tennessee and Louisiana coins are erroneously depicted and have the bell and leadpipe on the same side as the instruments' valves. This gives the

Tennessee quarter the distinction of being a "two error" design. These errors were noted by Michele Orzano in "Details Matter," a state quarters column about design inaccuracy (*Coin World*, March 25, 2002).

FACTS AND FIGURES

Reverse design: A collage at the center including a trumpet (this was a year for trumpets, and one would also be used on the 2002 Louisiana quarter), a guitar with six strings, a violin (or fiddle), and a music book. Three large pointed stars are in an arc above and to the sides. Below, the inscription MUSICAL HERITAGE is on a ribbon. Other features are standard.

Reverse designed by: Someone on the Mint staff, identity not disclosed.

Die created by Mint sculptor-engraver: Donna Weaver

Engraver's initials and location: DW. Above the ribbon end at the right.

Statehood date: June 1, 1796

Official coin release date: January 2, 2002 • On January 14, 2002, the launch ceremony was held at the Country Music Hall of Fame in Nashville, with state dignitaries and Treasury and Mint officials on hand. Afterward there was an open house at the State Capitol.

Circulation strike mintage (clad composition) • 2002-P Tennessee: 361,600,000 • **2002-D Tennessee:** 286,468,000. • This is the lowest Denver figure to this time. • The total of 648,068,000 from both mints was the lowest in the state series to this time, a situation attributed to a slowdown in the national economy and a consequently reduced call for coins in circulation.

Proof mintage (clad composition) • 2002-S Tennessee: 3,039,320

Proof mintage (silver composition) • 2002-S Tennessee: 888,826

2002 ᐧ OHIO

T he history of the 2002 Ohio quarter is especially well documented as numismatist Tom Noe chaired the committee evaluating the designs, and among the members were *Coin World* editor Beth Deisher and Bill Kamb, president of the Columbus Numismatic Society.

The coin was described as follows by the United States Mint:

> The Ohio quarter, the second quarter of 2002 and seventeenth in the series, honors the state's contribution to the history of aviation, depicting an early aircraft and an astronaut, superimposed as a group on the outline of the state. The design also includes the inscription "Birthplace of Aviation Pioneers."

The claim to this inscription is well justified—the history making astronauts Neil Armstrong and John Glenn were both born in Ohio, as was Orville Wright, co-inventor of the airplane. Orville and his brother, Wilbur Wright, also built and tested one of their early aircraft, the 1905 *Flyer III*, in Ohio.

Originally, the committee had recommended BIRTHPLACE OF AVIATION as the inscription on the coin, this matching what was on Ohio state license plates. On the coin this was changed to BIRTHPLACE OF AVIATION PIONEERS. The Commission of Fine Arts had suggested the change, as there was some question as to where aviation was actually "born" (the first flight had taken place in North Carolina and had already been depicted on the quarter of that state). The *Toledo Blade* reported that the astronaut depicted was created at the Mint by using a photograph taken by Neil Armstrong of Colonel Edwin "Buzz" Aldrin, Jr.—a clear violation of Mint rules that no living person be used as a motif. Accordingly, an alteration was made.

The Ohio quarter launch ceremony was held at the United States Air Force Museum located on the Wright-Patterson Air Force Base. Adjacent to the museum is Huffman Prairie Flying Field, where the Wright brothers successfully mastered the mechanics of controlled, powered, heavier-than-air flight in 1904 and 1905.

More than 1,000 people were on hand to participate in the launch ceremony. Among those who spoke were Stephen Wright, a descendant of the Wright brothers; astronauts John H. Glenn, Jr., and Neil Armstrong, both born in Ohio; Governor Bob Taft; and Mint Director Henrietta Holsman Fore. Donna Weaver, the U.S. Mint sculptor-engraver who created the coin model, also attended.

Commenting on the competition between North Carolina and Ohio in the honoring of the Wright brothers on their coins, Neil Armstrong said during the ceremony, "Both states can take justifiable pride: Ohio had the intellect and North Carolina had the wind."

FACTS AND FIGURES

Reverse design: The Wright *Flyer* against an outline map of Ohio, high in the air with a pilot seated at the controls. BIRTHPLACE OF AVIATION PIONEERS appears in three lines below. To the lower right is an astronaut, apparently "Buzz" Aldrin, standing in a space suit on the moon, facing forward. Other features are standard.

Reverse designed by: Identity not publicized.

Die created by Mint sculptor-engraver: Donna Weaver

Engraver's initials and location: DW. Below the lower left side of the map.

Statehood date: March 1, 1803

Official coin release date: March 11, 2002 (coins released into the Federal Reserve system). The launch ceremony was held a week later on March 18, 2002.

Circulation strike mintage (clad composition) • 2002-P Ohio: 217,200,000. This is the lowest quantity for any circulation strike variety of any state quarter, from any mint, to this time. The Philadelphia Mint was closed for nearly six of the normal 10 weeks in the standard production period, to remedy violations pointed out by the Occupational Safety and Health Administration (OSHA). • **2002-D Ohio:** 414,832,000

Proof mintage (clad composition) • 2002-S Ohio: 3,039,320

Proof mintage (silver composition) • 2002-S Ohio: 888,826

2002 · LOUISIANA

The 2002 Louisiana quarter features a textured area indicating the Louisiana Purchase as a part of an outline map of the United States, the acquisition having been made for a cost of $15,000,000 in 1803, during the presidency of Thomas Jefferson. The brown pelican, the state bird of Louisiana, is also depicted, as is a trumpet and musical notes—honoring the tradition of jazz in New Orleans.

This was the result of considerable effort, beginning in a significant way when the governor established the Louisiana Commemorative Coin Advisory Commission which eventually reviewed 1,193 design suggestions (about 80% of which were submitted by schoolchildren). Five concepts were given to the United States Mint, which developed designs. Governor Mike Foster, Jr., made the final choice, not at all his first choice, which had been "a peli-

can facing right roosting on a pier piling and a paddlewheel riverboat traveling west over an outline of the state."

In a 2003 article web site, *Coin World* columnist Michele Orzano said this motif didn't play out very well:

> One design that doesn't "work," or offers a mixed message at best, is the 2002 Louisiana quarter dollar design. The coin features the outline of a map of the United States with a highlighted area designating the Louisiana Purchase and text stating LOUISIANA PURCHASE. That's a message all by itself, but the design gets complicated because a pelican is depicted below the map and a trumpet with musical notes is depicted above the map.

In this instance, it seems that the state lost and the Mint won.

The state emblem of Louisiana, here depicted on a National Bank of Baton Rouge stock certificate, features a brown pelican, also seen on the state quarter.

FACTS AND FIGURES

Reverse design: A full outline of the contiguous 48 United States is shown, with the Louisiana Purchase Territory represented in a stippled map (with no topological features), protruding slightly above what is presently the border, as shown, of the country. At the bottom of the stippled area a line separates what is now the state of Louisiana. Above is a trumpet with three musical notes, to the right is the inscription LOUISIANA PURCHASE, and to the lower left is a standing brown pelican, apparently with its beak empty. Other features are standard.

Reverse designed by: Identity not publicized.

Die created by Mint sculptor-engraver: John Mercanti

Engraver's initials and location: JM. In the Gulf of Mexico below where Pensacola, FL, is (but not indicated).

Statehood date: April 30, 1812

Official coin release date: May 20, 2002 • The launch ceremony was held on May 30, 2002, at the former New Orleans Mint at 400 Esplanade Avenue(used for coinage purposes 1838–1861 and again 1879–1909). On hand from the Mint were Director Henrietta Holsman Fore and Associate Director David Pickens, the latter chairing a collectors' forum immediately after the event.

Circulation strike mintage (clad composition) • **2002-P Louisiana:** 362,000,000 • **2002-D Louisiana:** 402,204,000

Proof mintage (clad composition) • **2002-S Louisiana:** 3,039,320

Proof mintage (silver composition) • **2002-S Louisiana:** 888,826

2002 · INDIANA

The Indiana quarter of 2000, representing the 19th state to join the Union, includes 19 stars as part of the motif. The primary image is an outline map of the state against which is set a racecar of the type used in the famous Indianapolis 500 races (held every year from 1911 to date, except during World Wars I and II). The angle and strength of the car image makes it appear to almost be speeding toward the viewer. The inscription CROSSROADS OF AMERICA reflects the status of the state as a focus of transportation.

Governor Frank O'Bannon asked his wife Judy to request designs for the quarter, this taking place at the Indiana State Fair on August 17, 1999. Eventually 3,737 ideas were received. The Indiana Quarter Design Committee selected 17 of these and submitted them to a referendum of state citizens. After tallying 160,000 responses, the committee selected four semi-finalists and sent them to the United States Mint.

The Mint reviewed the designs, made changes, and sent the revisions back to O'Bannon. On July 18, 2001, the governor made the final choice: a design based on 17-year-old Josh Harvey's concept, with some modifications. (The Commission of Fine Arts had recommended an entirely different design, one featuring Chief Little Turtle of the Miami Indian nation.)

"Josh did a great job capturing the images that people most identify with Indiana," the governor said in a press release. "Our love of basketball and motor racing is world-famous, and I think that when people see our quarter, they'll know immediately that it represents Indiana."

The launch ceremony was described by Michele Orzano on the *Coin World* web site:

> If you're an auto-racing fan and you missed the official release of Indiana's State quarter dollar August 8 you really missed a treat. Where else could you see a governor riding in a race car being driven by the youngest woman to ever compete in the Indianapolis 500, who just days after the ceremony became the first woman to win the pole position for a major Indy car race? When was the last time you saw a Brink's armored carrier sharing the same track as an Indy Racing League car and three high-powered Corvettes?

Also in attendance, as at all such ceremonies, were prominent state and Treasury Department officials.

FACTS AND FIGURES

Reverse design: A powerful Indianapolis 500 racecar against the top part of a stippled outline map (without topological features), facing forward and slightly right. CROSSROADS OF AMERICA is below. To the left are 18 stars arranged in a partial circle, with a stray star in the field within, making a total of 19, representing the order of the state's admission to the Union. Other features are standard.

Reverse designed by: Josh Harvey

Die created by Mint sculptor-engraver: Donna Weaver

Engraver's initials and location: DW. Below the lower right of the map.

Statehood date: December 11, 1816

Official coin release date: August 2, 2002, for the distribution date to the Federal Reserve System. The launching ceremony was held at the Indianapolis Motor Speedway on August 8, 2002.

Circulation strike mintage (clad composition) • 2002-P Indiana: 362,600,000 • **2002-D Indiana:** 327,200,000

Proof mintage (clad composition) • 2002-S Indiana: 3,039,320

Proof mintage (silver composition) • 2002-S Indiana: 888,826

2002 ⋅ MISSISSIPPI

The Mississippi quarter of 2002, with its bold treatment of the state flower (voted as such in 1952) and THE MAGNOLIA STATE inscription, is simple and effective in its concept—reflecting a tried and true symbol. Variety is the spice of life, and the reiteration of familiar motifs is not always desirable, but in this instance the depiction of *Magnolia grandiflora* scored an artistic success (although it is best appreciated by viewing close up, not at a distance).

Without saying much as to how the designs originated—all in the mind of the governor, or perhaps with outside input—the United States Mint gives this:

> In response to the United States Mint's request for design concepts for the Mississippi quarter, Governor Ronnie Musgrove submitted three concepts on June 22, 2000, a Magnolia flower with a branch, a

mockingbird and "Mississippi— The Magnolia State."

The United States Mint provided Governor Musgrove with three candidate designs from which he chose "The Magnolia State" on July 3, 2001.

Magnolias, steamboats, and the mighty Mississippi River: writer Mark Twain himself would probably approve of the attractive quarter of the Magnolia State.

FACTS AND FIGURES

Reverse design: Magnolia blossoms and leaves dominating, with *The Magnolia State* in italic letters in three lines at the above right. Other features are standard.

Reverse designed by: Identity not publicized.

Die created by Mint sculptor-engraver: Donna Weaver

Engraver's initials and location: DW. Incuse on the lowest leaf at the right; the first incuse signature in the state quarter series.

Statehood date: December 10, 1817

Official coin release date: October 15, 2002 • The launching ceremony was held on October 22, 2002 in Jackson, the state capital. Governor Ronnie Musgrove was among the state dignitaries in attendance.

Circulation strike mintage (clad composition) • 2002-P Mississippi: 290,000,000 • **2002-D Mississippi:** 289,600,000

Proof mintage (clad composition) • 2002-S Mississippi: 3,039,320

Proof mintage (silver composition) • 2002-S Mississippi: 888,826

2003 · ILLINOIS

A n outline map of Illinois sets the background for the design of this state's 2003 quarter. Abraham Lincoln as a young man is seen inside the map, while other motifs, quite diverse, include a farm and the Chicago skyline. Around the border are 21 stars, reflecting the state's sequence in joining the Union (on December 3, 1818). In 1918, the Illinois Centennial commemorative half dollar also featured Lincoln, but as a facial portrait.

In January 2001, Governor George Ryan launched the Governor's Classroom Contest, encouraging youngsters to submit ideas for the quarter. In time, more than 6,000 were submitted, of which about 5,700 were from schoolchildren. A 14-person committee then reviewed the suggestions and narrowed them down to three categories: state history; agriculture and industry; and symbols of the state. The Mint created five different designs from these, from which Governor Ryan made the final decision.

A clean-shaven and contemplative Abraham Lincoln resides on the 1918 Illinois Centennial half dollar. The coin was the first U.S. commemorative to honor a state's admission to the Union. Lincoln's portrait was taken from the statue by Andrew O'Connor (in Springfield), and the reverse was based on the design of the Illinois state seal.

FACTS AND FIGURES

Reverse design: An outline map of Illinois enclosing most of the standing figure of Abraham Lincoln, holding a book in his right hand and a small object in his left. *Land of Lincoln* is in three lines to the left, and *21st State Century* in three lines to the right, all in upper and lower case italic figures. At the upper left in the field are outlines of a farmhouse, barn, and silo. At the upper right is the outline of the Chicago skyline, dominated by the Sears Tower. At the left and right border, 21 stars represent the order in which the state was admitted to the Union. Other features are standard.

Reverse designed by: Identity not publicized.

Die created by Mint sculptor-engraver: Donna Weaver

Engraver's initials and location: DW. To the right of the bottom of the map. On some coins the initials are indistinct.

Statehood date: December 3, 1818

Official coin release date: January 2, 2003

Circulation strike mintage (clad composition) • 2003-P Illinois: 225,800,000 • **2003-D Illinois:** 237,400,000

Proof mintage (clad composition) • 2003-S Illinois: N/A

Proof mintage (silver composition) • 2003-S Illinois: N/A

2003 ‣ ALABAMA

The 2003 Alabama quarter design features Helen Keller (1880–1968), the world-famous author, lecturer, and Radcliffe College graduate (with honors), who lost her sight, hearing, and speech from illness at the age of 19 months. The coin features Keller's name in English as well as in Braille. At the sides are a long-leaf pine branch and magnolias, while SPIRIT OF COURAGE (inscribed on a banner) embodies the essence of Keller's life.

In 1819, Alabama joined the Union as the 22nd state. The 100th anniversary of this event was celebrated a bit late with the 1921 Alabama Centennial commemorative half dollar. The state is rich in other numismatic connections, including the early issues of Confederate States of America paper money, 1861, when Montgomery was the capital of the Confederacy (later relocated to Richmond, Virginia).

For the quarter design, Governor Don Siegelman called for schoolchildren to create ideas based on the theme "Education: Link to the Past, Gateway to the Future." From the entries received he selected topics including social movements in the state, social and economic history, and Helen Keller. Paul Gilkes, in an article from *Coin World*'s web site ("2003 State Quarter Designs Under Final Review"), notes that the Commission of Fine Arts and the Citizens Commemorative Coin Advisory Committee both preferred a design featuring the State Capitol in Montgomery, while the choice of the governor was a design "bearing state symbols."

Sketches were produced at the Mint, sent to the governor, and he made the final selection, one not among those favorites mentioned above.

A commemorative half dollar was struck in 1921 to celebrate Alabama's state centennial (which had actually occurred in 1919). The coins were first offered to the public during President Warren Harding's visit to Birmingham in October. The two men pictured on the half dollar are William Wyatt Bibb, the state's first governor, and T.E. Kilby, governor at the time of the centennial.

FACTS AND FIGURES

Reverse design: Three-quarters view of Helen Keller seated in a chair, facing to the right, with her fingers on the surface of a Braille book in her lap. SPIRIT *of* COURAGE is on a ribbon below. Her name appears in Braille in the field to the right, with HELEN KELLER in two lines immediately below it. A long leaf pine branch is at the left border and a magnolia branch is at the right border. Other features are standard.

Reverse designed by: Identity not publicized.

Die created by Mint sculptor-engraver: Norman E. Nemeth

Engraver's initials and location: NEN. In the field below SPI (in SPIRIT).

Statehood date: December 14, 1819

Official coin release date: March 10, 2003 (different from the announced date of March 17, 2003)

Circulation strike mintage (clad composition) • 2003-P Alabama: 225,000,000 • **2003-D Alabama:** 232,400,000

Proof mintage (clad composition) • 2003-S Alabama: N/A

Proof mintage (silver composition) • 2003-S Alabama: N/A

2003 · MAINE

The Maine quarter of 2003 was the last for the six New England States. The design shows a lighthouse on the rockbound Atlantic coast—Pemaquid Point Light in New Harbor, marking the entrance to Muscongos Bay and Johns Bay. The U.S. Mint notes that the lighthouse, built in 1826 and replaced in 1835, "is still a beacon for ships and remains one of Maine's most popular tourist attractions." The ship at right represents *Victory Chimes*, the last three-masted schooner of the windjammer fleet—another symbol of Maine's connection to the sea.

Maine became a state on March 15, 1820, under the Missouri Compromise—the attempted balancing of the Union by adding a state with freedom, to counterweigh the slaveholding state of Missouri. Previously Maine was a district of Massachusetts, separated from that state by New Hampshire.

The Commission on the Maine State Quarter Design was established by Governor Angus King in March 2001. More than 200 sketches and ideas were received. These were narrowed to just three and sent to the governor, who added a fourth. The candidates then stood as "Nation's First Light," "Where America's Day Begins," Mt. Katahdin, and the lighthouse at Pemaquid Point.

More than 100,000 citizens voted on the Maine sketches, and the Pemaquid lighthouse was the most popular.

Daniel J. Carr, a Colorado artist, submitted the lighthouse design. In its original form on the sketch it appeared as a bold structure on the right side of the coin, with rays streaming to the left and the right, a pine tree to the far right, and at sea to the left a three-masted schooner, Victory Chimes, a 170-foot ship in service since 1954. The motif was done in cooperation with Leland and Carolyn Pendleton of Rockland, Maine, the coastal port home of the Victory Chimes. This was done in technical conformity to the rules that the motif must be by a Maine resident.

FACTS AND FIGURES

Reverse design: The Pemaquid Lighthouse casting beams, on the left, high on the rocky shore. At its base is the fenced-in residential compound of the lighthouse keeper. At sea in the distance to the right is the three-masted schooner, *Victory Chimes*, with two seagulls nearby. Other features are standard.

Reverse designed by: Daniel J. Carr, with Leland and Carolyn Pendleton

Die created by Mint sculptor-engraver: Donna Weaver

Engraver's initials and location: DW. Incuse on a shore rock at the edge of the design at lower left.

Statehood date: March 15, 1820

Official coin release date: June 2, 2003, for release into circulation by the Federal Reserve System. • On June 9, the launch ceremony was held at the Pemaquid Lighthouse, New Harbor, with Governor John Elias Baldacci, Mint Director Henrietta Holsman Fore, Maine humorist Tim Sample, various lighthouse historians, and a few hundred others in attendance on a foggy and overcast day. It had been planned to have the *Victory Chimes* on hand, but the weather precluded this, although Captain Kip Files was there.

Circulation strike mintage (clad composition) • **2003-P Maine:** 217,400,000 • **2003-D Maine:** 231,400,000 • The combined mintage of 448,800,000 circulation strikes from these two mints represents the lowest in the statehood series to date, in contrast to 1,594,616,000 circulation strikes for the 2000 Virginia quarters, the high-level record holder to date.

Proof mintage (clad composition) • **2003-S Maine:** N/A

Proof mintage (silver composition) • **2003-S Maine:** N/A

2003 · MISSOURI

Governor Bob Holden named 12 citizens of the Missouri Commemorative Quarter Design Committee in February 2001. A competition was announced, a dozen semi-final motifs were chosen, a statewide vote was taken, and finally, the sketch by Paul Jackson, a Missouri artist, was selected.

The design of the 2003 Missouri quarter dollar erupted into controversy when artist Jackson found that the Mint grossly modified it without consultation. He stated: "Entrants were told that the winning design would appear on the reverse of Missouri's quarter. Now it appears as if the competition was nothing more than a hoax. The United States Mint never intended to use our designs."

In its original form the Gateway Arch at St. Louis was small in the distance, above the center, with a river in the foreground and wooded banks to each side. At the center was a canoe with Lewis and Clark paddling. At the time it did not attract much admiration in numismatic circles, and many found it "average" in quality.

The design was altered by the Mint to move the Arch to the center, to change the appearance of the riverbank trees, to substitute a heavy rowboat (a pirogue) with six men and an American flag, and to add the inscription CORPS OF DIS-COVERY and the dates 1804 and 2004.

The Mint revision was given to the Commission of Fine Arts for review. The Commission members "felt more comfortable with a design featuring a single theme rather than conflicting motifs." Jackson continued to protest the changes, and appeared widely to publcize his views, including on National Public

Radio and on CBS television's "Up to the Minute" news program.

Some further changes were made, the rowboat was revised to have just three men, etc., but essentially the Mint's version prevailed. The entire situation—a story with two sides to it, played out at length in the numismatic as well as the public press, was a first-class headache for just about everyone involved, creating a quarter that many observers found to be one of the poorest in the series. Mint Director Jay Johnson later remi-nisced (in a July 2004 conversation with the author), "I still remember the remark that the design looked like three men in a tub rowing between two clumps of broccoli!"

This regrettable controversy was the catalyst for the United States Mint revising its rules. Future quarter designs for 2005 and later would be created by the Mint itself, with concepts submitted in writing, and the Mint doing the artistry.

FACTS AND FIGURES

Reverse design: The Gateway Arch at St. Louis forming the center of the design, with three men in a pirogue in the water in front of it, headed toward the lower left. At each side are riverbanks with trees. Above is the inscription, CORPS OF DISCOVERY, and the dates 1804 and 2004. Other features are standard.

Reverse designed by: Paul Jackson. Original concept modified by the Mint.

Die created by Mint sculptor-engraver: Alfred F. Maletsky

Engraver's initials and location: A.M. In script capital letters in the field below the ground at the right.

Statehood date: August 10, 1821

Official coin release date: August 4, 2003 • The launch ceremony was held on August 10, 2003.

Circulation strike mintage (clad composition) • **2003-P Missouri:** 225,000,000 • **2003-D Missouri:** 228,200,000

Proof mintage (clad composition) • **2003-S Missouri:** N/A

Proof mintage (silver composition) • **2003-S Missouri:** N/A

2003 · ARKANSAS

The Arkansas quarter of 2003 features a collage of items relating to the state, including a cut diamond, rice stalks, a lake, and a mallard. The suite is arranged to be heavy at the sides, and light at the middle, somewhat distracting to the eyes of some observers. The Mint described the design:

> It is fitting that the "Natural State," Arkansas's official nickname, chose images of natural resources. Arkansas has an abundance of clear streams, rivers and lakes. In fact, Arkansas has more than 600,000 acres of natural lakes. Arkansas is also known for its sportsmanship and boasts mallard hunting as a main attraction for hunters across the nation.
>
> Visitors to Arkansas can search Crater of Diamonds State Park for precious gems including, of course,

diamonds. The mine at Crater of Diamonds State Park reportedly is the oldest diamond mine in North America, and the only one in the United States open to the public. Visitors get to keep what they find.

Visitors can also experience "rice fever" in Arkansas—just the way W.H. Fuller did when he grew the first commercially successful rice crop in Arkansas. Soon after, thousands of acres of the Grand Prairie were changed to cultivate rice, and Arkansas became the leading producer of the grain in the United States.

The search for a design was launched by Governor Mike Huckabee in January 2001, under the name of the Arkansas Quarter Challenge. In two weeks 9,320 entries were received. The field was subsequently narrowed to three, whose creators each received $1,000 in cash. The Mint then made its own sketches and submitted them to the governor, and he made the final choice. The motif of Ariston Jacks, modified at the Mint, was the winner.

Numismatists may remember that decades ago, beginning in 1935, Arkansas celebrated its 1836–1936 centennial with a series of commemorative half dollars.

The 1935 Arkansas half dollar featured portraits of an Indian chief of 1836 and an American girl of 1936. Another version, struck in 1936, showed Senator Joseph T. Robinson.

FACTS AND FIGURES

Reverse design: A collage of Arkansas-iana greeting the eye, with a faceted diamond in the air above a group of pine trees, and a marsh or lake in the foreground. A mallard duck to the right, with wings upraised, seems to be rising (for its feet are not extended, as they would be if it were about to alight on the water). To the left are stalks of rice. The motif is unique to this point in time in that it includes no motto or sentiment apart from the required state name, dates, and E PLURIBUS UNUM. Other features are standard.

Reverse designed by: Ariston Jacks of Pine Bluff, Arkansas

Die created by Mint sculptor-engraver: John Mercanti

Engraver's initials and location: JM. Incuse on a raised water detail at the lower right.

Statehood date: June 15, 1836

Official coin release date: October 20, 2003 • The launch ceremony was held on October 28, 1003, at the Crater of Diamonds State Park in Murfreesboro. Local schoolchildren were given "free samples."

Circulation strike mintage (clad composition) • 2003-P Arkansas: 228,000,000 • **2003-D Arkansas:** 229,800,000

Proof mintage (clad composition) • 2003-S Arkansas: N/A

Proof mintage (silver composition) • 2003-S Arkansas: N/A

2004 · MICHIGAN

The Michigan quarter of 2004 is similar in concept to the Cleveland Centennial commemorative half dollar of 1936, in that both have outline maps of the five Great Lakes as the central theme. Some observers thought that an automobile would be more representative of the state. Michigan borders on four of these lakes and, per Mint publicity, "Standing anywhere in the state, a person is within 85 miles of one of the Great Lakes."

Actually, a motor car was indeed among the four also-ran semi-finalists, these being "Michigan State Outline, with Great Lakes and State Icons," "Michigan State Outline, with Great Lakes and the Mackinac Bridge," "Michigan State Outline, with the Mackinac Bridge and Automobile," and "Michigan State Outline, with Great Lakes and Automobile." These and other ideas were among over 4,300 submitted to the Michigan Quarter Commission. Governor Jennifer Engler

selected the winner in September 2003. The final design engendered quite a bit of controversy, both in numismatic periodicals and in Michigan newspapers. Among various state designs, it seemed to be among the least pleasing.

One observer, Ken Anderson, wrote this to *Coin World:*

> I congratulate Governor Jennifer Granholm in regards to the Michigan State quarter design. Her comment of the state outline being the most recognizable characteristic when viewed from space is not justification for portraying only the outline on our quarter.
>
> Out of the first 50 quarters the Michigan quarter is the only quarter that does not depict something of interest within the state, the people of Michigan, or any major accomplishments of its citizens. Next time we are all in space we must remember to look for the outline of Michigan.

Tuebor, the Latin motto on this 1876 depiction of the Michigan seal, means "I will defend." The ship at right illustrates the importance of the Great Lakes maritime trade to the state's prosperity.

FACTS AND FIGURES

Reverse design: An outline map of the five Great Lakes dominating the center, with the state of Michigan set apart in bas-relief seemingly representing actual topology. GREAT LAKES STATE is in three lines to the upper left. Other features are standard.

Reverse designed by: Identity not publicized.

Die created by Mint sculptor-engraver: Donna Weaver

Engraver's initials and location: DW. On the Ohio shore (not indicated as such) on the southern edge of Lake Erie.

Statehood date: January 26, 1837

Official coin release date: January 26, 2004 • On the appointed date the quarter was unveiled in the rotunda of the State Capitol building in Lansing as about 400 watched. The program included several speakers: Mint Director Henrietta Holsman Fore; Governor Jennifer Granholm; and Richard Watts (president of the Michigan State Numismatic Society).

Circulation strike mintage (clad composition) • **2004-P Michigan:** 233,800,000 • **2004-D Michigan:** 225,800,000 (lowest Denver Mint production to this time for a state quarter). Many show lightly struck details.

Proof mintage (clad composition) • **2004-S Michigan:** N/A

Proof mintage (silver composition) • **2004-S Michigan:** N/A

2004 ⋅ FLORIDA

Illustrating a Spanish galleon along with other motifs, the 2004 Florida quarter is one of the few to include a distinctly numismatic scene, in this case indirectly. Centuries ago the Spanish treasure fleet, typically consisting of a dozen or more vessels, returned from possessions in the New World, bearing gold and silver coins and ingots for the royal coffers. The typical homeward route called for a rendezvous at Havana, then passage northward along the east coast of Florida, then into the broad Atlantic. During the so-called equinoctial storms, now known as the late summer and early autumn hurricane season, certain of these ships perished, including virtually the entire fleets of 1715 and 1733. Many coins have been recovered from the remains of these vessels, to the delight of the collecting community.

Officially the motif on the 2004 quarter was given as GATEWAY TO DIS-COVERY, certainly applicable to the space shuttle also depicted. Further shown is a detached strip of land with Sabal palm trees. The 1935 Old Spanish Trail commemorative half dollar, with a map of the southern states, is related—the trail began in Florida and was taken westward by adventurers and explorers. The name of the state was given by an explorer, Ponce de Leon, who on Easter 1513 named the district Pascua Florida, or "Flowery Easter."

To get the coin project underway, Governor Jeb Bush appointed a nine-person Florida Commemorative Quarter Committee on April 9, 2002. In time more than 1,500 ideas were received, a field narrowed by the committee to 25, then to 10. These were sent to the governor, who selected five semi-finalists, with themes including "The Everglades," "Gateway to Discovery," "Fishing Capital of the World," "St. Augustine," and "America's Spaceport." The final choice was put to the vote of the citizens, who chose "Gateway to Discovery."

The 1935 Old Spanish Trail half dollar shows the trail from its starting point in Florida.

FACTS AND FIGURES

Reverse design: A Spanish galleon at the left and a shore with two palm trees to the right. GATEWAY TO DISCOVERY is below. Above the palm trees is a space shuttle at an angle, nose upward, as if coming in for a landing. Other features are standard.

Reverse designed by: Identity not publicized.

Die created by Mint sculptor-engraver: T. James Ferrell

Engraver's initials and location: TJF in italic capitals. On the shore below the rightmost palm tree.

Statehood date: March 3, 1845

Official coin release date: April 7, 2004 • There were two simultaneous launch ceremonies, the second such instance (after Massachusetts) in the state quarter series. The first was held at the Kennedy Space Center Visitor Complex in Cape Canaveral. Governor Jeb Bush, Mint Director Henrietta Holsman Fore, and NASA Administrator Sean O'Keefe were among the dignitaries in attendance. The other ceremony was staged about 100 miles to the north at Castillo de San Marcos, the ancient Spanish fort on the coast at St. Augustine, where Lt. Governor Toni Jennings was the ranking official on hand. The St. Augustine event was held in view of the fact that the quarter design featuring that city came in second place in the selection process.

Circulation strike mintage (clad composition) • **2004-P Florida:** 240,200,000 • **2004-D Florida:** 241,600,000 • Of the combined production from these two mints, more than 11,000,000 were sold at a premium in the form of rolls, 100-coin mini-bags, and 1,000-coin bags.

Proof mintage (clad composition) • **2004-S Florida:** N/A

Proof mintage (silver composition) • **2004-S Florida:** N/A

2004 · TEXAS

The Republic of Texas, which had used the lone star emblem on its flag beginning in 1839, joined the Union in 1845, becoming the 28th state. Its state quarter reflects this tradition, with an outline map of the state, a large single star, and the inscription, THE LONE STAR STATE. Around the border are two sections of rope symbolizing the cattle and cowboy tradition of Texas.

There was no lack of motifs to consider, what with the Alamo, oil wells, longhorn steer, armadillos, and chili cookouts! It is an interesting fact that the district has been under the flags of Spain, France, Mexico, the Republic of Texas, the United States of America, the Confederate States of America, and the U.S.A. again, which equates to six *different*, giving rise to the Six Flags amusement park in the late 20th century, which eventually expanded to use the name in other states. The state name is derived from *Tejas*, an Indian word meaning *friends*, a logical connection to the present-day motto, Friendship.

In August 14, 2000, Governor George W. Bush, with his eye on the November presidential election, found time to appoint 15 people to the Texas Quarter Dollar Coin Advisory Committee. This group enlisted the Texas Numismatic Association to supervise a contest which resulted in more than 2,500 ideas submitted (these only from natives of the state or those who had lived there for at least a year as of May 11, 2001, the start of the competition). The association selected 17 finalists and submitted them to the committee, and five semi-finalists emerged. Governor Rick Perry selected the winner: a sketch made by Daniel Miller, a graphic artist from Arlington, Texas.

The Alamo, seen here in an 1894 photograph from James Cox's *Our Own Country*, is among the most famous Texas landmarks. Although it has been the subject of various tokens and commemorative medals over the years, the fort has never been depicted on a circulating U.S. coin.

FACTS AND FIGURES

Reverse design: A bold five-pointed star, with ridges to each ray, against a stippled map of the state (with no topological features). In the field to the lower left is THE LONE STAR STATE in three lines, in upper and lower case block letters. Arc-like sections of rope appear individually to the left and right, representing a lariat. Other features are standard.

Reverse designed by: Daniel Miller, a graphic artist from Arlington

Die created by Mint sculptor-engraver: Norman E. Nemeth

Engraver's initials and location: NEN. Located in the Gulf of Mexico (not specifically indicated) to the right of the lower tip of the state.

Statehood date: December 29, 1845

Official coin release date: June 10, 2004, official hour and minute stated as 9:30 a.m., at the Bob Bullock Texas History Museum in Austin.

Circulation strike mintage (clad composition) • **2004-P Texas:** N/A • **2004-D Texas:** N/A

Proof mintage (clad composition) • **2004-S Texas:** N/A

Proof mintage (silver composition) • **2004-S Texas:** N/A

2004 · IOWA

The Iowa quarter design of 2004 features a one-room schoolhouse with a teacher and students planting a large tree, a motif based on an obscure and somewhat surrealistic painting, *Arbor Day*, by Grant Wood (an Iowa-born artist best known for *American Gothic*, with its stern-visaged farm couple facing forward, the man holding a pitchfork, with a farmhouse in the background). Inscriptions reading FOUNDATION IN EDUCATION and GRANT WOOD are part of the design. On the coin, many of the original painting's details are altered, including the omission of the school outhouse (privy) and the addition of a seemingly very large tree (about ten feet high) with a root clump that must weigh hundreds of pounds—in real life a bit heavy for little schoolchildren to move around!

The connection with education does not seem particularly unique to Iowa, and many felt that a cornfield would have been a better selection. At any rate, the Mint did make a connection, noting that Iowa already had a number of rural country schools in each county by the time it became a state, and established its first high school in the 1850s, about 50 years ahead of most of the rest of the country. The Mint also noted that "Although Iowa has long been a leader in agriculture, the state is unique in that it is the only one whose east and west borders are completely formed by rivers— the Mississippi and Missouri rivers."

Finding "unique claims" for each state provides fun reading for numismatists today. We learn not only of the one-of-a-kind river situation described above, but also, for example, that in Michigan no one can stand anywhere without being within 85 miles of one of the Great Lakes.

Governor Thomas J. Vilsack set up the Iowa Quarter Commission, with 16 members, who selected libraries, banks, and credit unions as information gathering sources for the designs submitted—nearly 2,000 ideas in all. These were narrowed down to five themes: "American Gothic," "Foundation in Education," "Feeding the World," "Sullivan Brothers," and "Beautiful Land." A fair amount of controversy ensued. Certain of the five Sullivan brothers of Waterloo (who died heroically in November 1942 when their ship, the *U.S.S. Juneau*, was sunk) were considered by some as juvenile delinquents before they went into service. Other committee members wanted corn and only corn ("Feeding the World"), and still others demanded *American Gothic*. It was Governor Vilsack who settled the question and picked his favorite as the winner.

FACTS AND FIGURES

Reverse design: A one-room clapboard schoolhouse at the center and left. To the right, a teacher and several children planting a tree. In the distance can be seen a road, fence, and undulating farmland. The legend, FOUNDATION IN EDUCATION, is at the upper right. Grant Wood's name appears more prominently than on any other United States legal tender coin ever minted, seemingly a contradiction of Mint policy not to feature the name of the designer, but honor only the Mint engraver.

Reverse designed by: Adapted from a painting by Grant Wood.

Die created by Mint sculptor-engraver: John Mercanti

Engraver's initials and location: JM. In the lower left field of the design.

Statehood date: December 28, 1846

Official coin release date: August 30, 2004, at noon • A ceremonial striking ceremony for the 2004-D quarters was held at 2 p.m., July 12, 2004, at the Denver Mint. On hand were State Treasurer Michael L. Fitzgerald (who chaired the Iowa Quarter Commission), Denver Mint Plant Manager Tim Riley, and others. • For the Philadelphia quarters, *Coin World* (July 19, 2004) reported: "September 3 will be the ceremonial kick-off date for the 2004 Iowa quarter dollars. Governor Tom Vilsack will attend the ceremony, whose location has not been finalized. Officials say the event will occur either at the Iowa Statehouse or the Iowa State Fairgrounds. It's possible that a second ceremony would take place in Vilsack's hometown of Mount Pleasant."

Circulation strike mintage (clad composition) • **2004-P Iowa:** 213,800,000 • **2004-D Iowa:** 251,800,000

Proof mintage (clad composition) • **2004-S Iowa:** N/A

Proof mintage (silver composition) • **2004-S Iowa:** N/A

2004 · WISCONSIN

The Wisconsin quarter of 2004, number 30 in the 50-state series, features an agricultural theme, with the head of a cow and a wheel of cheese echoing the state motto, "America's Dairyland" (another motto, FORWARD, was actually used on the coin). An ear of corn is also depicted. Mint publicity included this:

> Wisconsin adopted the state motto, "Forward," in 1851, reflecting Wisconsin's continuous drive to be a national leader. Wisconsin is the dairy capital of the world, ranking first in the number of milk cows and the production of over 15 percent of the nation's milk—more than any other state. Today, Wisconsin produces over 350 different varieties, types and styles of award-winning cheeses. There are approximately 17,000 dairy farms, with just over one million cows that

produce an average of 17,306 gallons of milk each, per year.

Wisconsin is also a major corn-growing state. In 2002, Wisconsin led the nation in corn silage production and, with 391.5 million bushels produced, it ranked fifth in the production of corn for grain (shelled corn). State corn production contributed $882.4 million to the Wisconsin economy in 2003. Wisconsin is also a leading supplier of meat.

In December 2001, Governor Scott McCallum named 23 people to the Wisconsin Commemorative Quarter Council. Over the allotted period of time for submissions 9,608 ideas were received, which the committee narrowed to six, further reduced (by a statewide referendum) to these: "Scenic Wisconsin," "Agriculture/Dairy/Barns," and "Early Exploration and Cultural Interaction." In 2003, Governor Jim Doyle submitted these to the choice of voters, and "Agriculture/Dairy/Barns" was the winner.

Coin collectors in early 2005 discovered that there are two uncommon varieties of the Wisconsin quarter design. The "Extra Leaf, High" and "Extra Leaf, Low" varieties have an extra leaf in the corn husk, on the left side of the ear.

So far nobody has determined how these variations came to exist, or even whether they're from damaged coinage dies or a deliberate prank played at the Mint. Whatever the case, check your pocket change—no matter how they happened, they're worth a lot more than 25 cents to collectors!

Old Milwaukee is seen in this river view from 1876, bustling with activity and commerce.

FACTS AND FIGURES

Reverse design: The head of a cow (wearing a cowbell) to the left, facing right, with its nose nearly touching a large wheel of cheese from which a section has been cut. Behind the cheese is a vertical, unshucked ear of corn. FORWARD is on a ribbon at the bottom of the design. Other features are standard.

Reverse designed by: Identity not publicized.

Die created by Mint sculptor-engraver: Alfred F. Maletsky

Engraver's initials and location: AM. In the field below D (in FORWARD).

Circulation strike mintage (clad composition) • 2004-P Wisconsin: 226,400,00 • **2004-D Wisconsin:** 226,800,000

Proof mintage (clad composition) • 2004-S Wisconsin: N/A

Proof mintage (silver composition) • 2004-S Wisconsin: N/A

2005 · CALIFORNIA

Much interest was centered on the selection of a motif for California's quarter in 2004, a year in advance. More than 8,000 design entries were made. Semi-finalists included the Golden Gate Bridge (familiar to numismatists from its bold portrayal on a 1936 commemorative half dollar), a gold miner (no doubt to be a hands-down winner in the view of most all numismatists and those with a sense of history), John Muir and the Yosemite Valley, waves and the sun, and the giant sequoia tree. Among the Gold Rush themes, none seemed to have a dynamic quality. Moreover, many citizens said that the subject had been overdone on earlier commemoratives.

The Treasury Department made its approval on April 15, 2004, and Governor Arnold Schwarzenegger announced that the forthcoming 2005 state quarter would feature not the Gold Rush, nor the Golden Gate, nor the Bear Flag. Instead, John Muir, the accomplished naturalist and writer, was to be depicted against a background of Yosemite National Park.

The Yosemite design, by Los Angeles artist Garrett Burke, is well balanced and artistically attractive, with its depiction of John Muir gazing at a broad view of the valley, famous for its Half Dome (the monolithic granite headwall dominating the design's right field), El Capitan, and Bridal Veil Falls. A California condor soars at center.

The coin became a reality with its official unveiling on March 2, accompanied by this news release from the governor:

"I have selected the John Muir Yosemite design to send to the U.S. Mint. This, basically, is a design that tells the whole story.

California's commemorative quarter will display John Muir, Yosemite National Park, and the California condor. John Muir, for instance, has been a model for generations of Californians and conservationists around the world. He has taught us to be active and to enjoy, but at the same time protect, our parks, our beaches, and our mountains. Yosemite is also on the coin, which is the symbol of California's beauty, and at the same time it reminds us that we must protect this beauty. Also on the coin is the California condor, which once almost was extinct and now is protected and has had an amazing comeback. Here in California, growth, progress, wilderness protection, and the protection of the environment go hand in hand. Even though some people believe that you can only have one or the other, we want to be committed to make it go hand in hand. I am proud that these three images will show California's wildlife, our majestic landscape, and our commitment to preserving our golden state for future generations."

Quickly, the new quarter became a numismatic favorite, with enthusiastic acclaim throughout the hobby. Designer Garrett Burke, his wife Michelle, and their daughter presented several programs to coin-collecting groups, and at the American Numismatic Association convention in San Francisco in July 2005, they tended a special exhibit illustrating the design and its background.

FACTS AND FIGURES

Reverse design: John Muir standing before a scene of Yosemite National Park, with a California condor flying in the sky. The legends JOHN MUIR and YOSEMITE VALLEY are to the left and right. Other features are standard.

Reverse designed by: Garrett Burke

Die created by Mint sculptor-engraver: Alfred Maletsky (finalizer of design); Don Everhart II (maker of model).

Engraver's initials and location: DE. Below the tree line at right.

Circulation strike mintage (clad composition) • 2004-P California: N/A • 2004-D California: N/A

Proof mintage (clad composition) • 2004-S California: N/A

Proof mintage (silver composition) • 2004-S California: N/A

2005 · MINNESOTA

The Minnesota Quarter Dollar Commission was set up to review design ideas for the state's quarter—the second to be released in 2005. On May 14, 2004, Governor Tim Pawlenty announced the commission's final choice, a fishing scene on a Minnesota lake. This beat out designs described as "State with Symbols" (including the state outline, a snowflake, a loon, and a plow); and "Mississippi River Headwaters."

"When people from around the world see our quarter," commented the governor (quoted in Numismatic News, June 1, 2004), "they will immediately associate Minnesota with the beautiful woods and waters of our natural resources."

The state, called the Land of 10,000 Lakes, is actually home to more than 15,000 lakes, with shoreline exceeding 90,000 miles (more than that of California, Florida, and Hawaii combined).

Minnesota is also the source of the headwaters of the Mississippi River.

The U.S. Mint describes the state:

> The natural beauty of Minnesota is vividly depicted on the reverse of this new quarter-dollar. Lined with Norway Pine, many of the lakes throughout the State offer much in the way of outdoor recreation, as well as providing a home for the graceful loon, Minnesota's state bird. Minnesota is also home to the Boundary Waters Canoe Area Wilderness. This one-million-acre wilderness area was established by Congress in 1978, and contains more than 1,500 miles of canoe routes and nearly 2,200 designated campsites.

The state emblem of Minnesota, as seen in this 1876 illustration, offers a "Wild West" scene of Indians and farmers living side by side, with cattle and a frontier cowboy added for good measure.

FACTS AND FIGURES

Reverse design: Lake scene with a loon in the foreground, a motorboat with two fishermen not far away to the right, and a shore wooded with pines in the distance. Somewhat incongruously a map of the state is placed vertically in the lake, to the left of the boat, and bears the inscription, LAND OF 10,000 LAKES. Other features are standard.

Die created by Mint sculptor-engraver: Charles Vickers

Engraver's initials and location: CLV. In the lake grass to the right of the loon.

Official coin release date: The launch ceremony was held on April 12, 2005, at the State Capitol in St. Paul. • The first official day of recording coin orders at the U.S. Mint was April 4.

Circulation strike mintage (clad composition) • 2005-P Minnesota: N/A • 2005-D Minnesota: N/A

Proof mintage (clad composition) • 2005-S Minnesota: N/A

Proof mintage (silver composition) • 2005-S Minnesota: N/A

2005 · OREGON

In the summer of 2003, Governor Ted Kulongski received many suggestions for coin motifs for his state—Mount Hood, salmon, Tom McCall, a woman, Crater Lake, a lighthouse, and Sacagawea among them, this per his press secretary, Mary Ellen Glynn. In the meantime he was selecting candidates to sit on the 18-member Oregon Commemorative Coin Commission, "which will include a high school teacher, a numismatist, a member of an Oregon tribe, a historian, a student, a Republican and a Democrat from both the state Senate and state House, the state treasurer and the governor himself." (*The Portland Tribune*, August 19, 2003)

On May 24, 2004, the governor endorsed the choice of the Commission and announced that Crater Lake would form the motif. An account in *Coin World* (June 14, 2003) told this:

The Crater Lake design features a view of the lake from the south rim, with conifer trees in the foreground, Wizard Island rising from the lake waters and the opposite rim. Crater Lake is the caldera of a volcano, Mount Mazama; the lake was formed following a cataclysmic eruption approximately 7,700 years ago. The lake is the deepest in the United States and seventh deepest in the world.

"Crater Lake is one of the natural wonders in the world. Steeped in thousands of years of history, and considered sacred land to the Native Americans, it is Oregon's only national park enjoyed by thousands every year," Kulongoski said in a news release. "Crater Lake represents all that is good in Oregon: beautiful scenery and a hardiness that is represented in its citizenry."

Crater Lake was one of four design concepts for Oregon. The other three designs show a Chinook salmon leaping up a waterfall, a snow-capped Mount Hood, and a covered wagon traveling past an American Indian encampment.

Kulongoski, who served as co-chair of the commission, said;

"The commission did a fantastic job of capturing Oregon in each of the four designs they submitted to me. All of the designs serve as a reminder of the great beauty and wonder we enjoy across our state and I appreciate the time they've given to this important project."

Wildlife, agriculture, and the ocean all figure into Oregon's state emblem.

FACTS AND FIGURES

Reverse design: A bird's-eye view of Crater Lake, the deepest lake in the United States, seen from the southwest rim. Other visible landmarks include Wizard Island, as well as the peaks known as Watchman and Hillman, and surrounding conifers. The legend CRATER LAKE completes the design.

Die created by Mint sculptor-engraver: Donna Weaver.

Engraver's initials and location: DW. At the trunk of the rightmost tree.

Official coin release date: The launch ceremony was held on June 15, 2005, in front of the Oregon State Historical Society in Portland. Dignitaries included Governor Ted Kulongoski and Gloria Eskridge, the U.S. Mint associate director. • June 6 was the official first day for orders at the U.S. Mint.

Circulation strike mintage (clad composition) • 2005-P Oregon: N/A • **2005-D Oregon:** N/A

Proof mintage (clad composition) • 2005-S Oregon: N/A

Proof mintage (silver composition) • 2005-S Oregon: N/A

2005 · KANSAS

In June 2003, Kansas Governor Kathleen Sebelius announced the creation of the 16-member Kansas Commemorative Coin Commission. Its goal was to narrow down the search for the state's quarter design to four finalists. The winner came from among a group of semi-finalist entries, many of which showed bison or their heads, wheat, sunflowers, and outline maps of the state. One had a sunflower with a banner across it labeled, "There's no place like home." Another, with a farmer in overalls standing in a sea of wheat with two children, was flatly rejected by the United States Mint and was eliminated from final consideration. The winning design was recommended by the state's high school students in a vote held the following spring. In addition to the winning design, finalists included the statue atop the State Capitol (an American Indian aiming his bow toward the North Star); a sunflower and wheat; and a single central sunflower.

The Department of Treasury approved the "Buffalo and Sunflower" design on July 13, 2004.

Featured was a standing bison, popularly but incorrectly called a "buffalo" by some, with a group of sunflowers to the left. No special inscriptions beyond the standard were shown on a publicized sketch. Curiously, the horns of the animal were pointing forward, "but as any bison rancher knows, the horns should be pointing up," one observer commented (Don Carbaugh, in *Numismatist*, August 2004). State officials suggested some modifications, including raising the bison's head, fixing the horn problem, and making the ground appear more natural.

The U.S. Mint's literature describes the scene:

> The Kansas commemorative quarter incorporates two of the state's most beloved symbols, the state animal and flower, the buffalo and the sunflower. Each of these two design elements is a visual reminder of our nation's heartland. They feature prominently in the history of the territory, and both were found in abundance throughout the state in the middle of the 19th century when Kansas gained its statehood. With its release in the fall of 2005, it is the second United States circulating coin of 2005 to carry an image of the buffalo.

FACTS AND FIGURES

Reverse design: An American bison stands on a small patch of ground, facing forward and slightly to the right. To the left are three large sunflowers. Other features are standard.

Die created by Mint sculptor-engraver: Norman Nemeth.

Engraver's initials and location: NEN. In the grass below the bison's head.

Circulation strike mintage (clad composition) • **2005-P Kansas:** N/A • **2005-D Kansas:** N/A

Proof mintage (clad composition) • **2005-S Kansas:** N/A

Proof mintage (silver composition) • **2005-S Kansas:** N/A

2005 · WEST VIRGINIA

More than 1,800 design concepts were submitted for the West Virginia quarter. Students from the Governor's School for the Arts narrowed this quantity down to five finalists. They included "Appalachian Warmth," "Bridge Day/New River Gorge," "River Rafters," "Mother's Day/Anna Jarvis," and "New River Gorge Bridge."

In March 2004, Governor Bob Wise announced that a depiction of the New River Gorge would be the design he submitted to the Treasury for the 2005 West Virginia quarter dollar. A sketch showed the river in the foreground and in the distance a steel bridge arching over forested slopes to each side of the waterway. The Treasury announced its approval of the design that summer.

The U.S. Mint describes the significance of the Gorge and its bridge thus:

The design chosen to represent West Virginia is one that combines the natural physical beauty of the State and the triumph of the human intellect exemplified by the engineering wonder that is the New River Gorge Bridge. At 3,030 feet long and 69 feet wide, the bridge is the world's largest steel span and the second highest bridge in the United States, rising 876 feet above the New River Gorge in southern West Virginia. In 1978, 53 miles of the New River was added to the National Park System as the New River Gorge National River.

Harpers Ferry is located where the Potomac and Shenandoah rivers meet, in the states of West Virginia, Maryland, and Virginia. Among the Americans whose histories cross this famous area are presidents George Washington and Thomas Jefferson, explorer Meriwether Lewis, abolitionists John Brown and Frederick Douglass, and Confederate war hero "Stonewall" Jackson.

FACTS AND FIGURES

Reverse design: A long view of the New River Gorge Bridge, with the gorge below. Legend NEW RIVER GORGE in the river's water. Other features are standard.

Die created by Mint sculptor-engraver: John Mercanti

Engraver's initials and location: JM. To the right of legend NEW RIVER GORGE.

Circulation strike mintage (clad composition) • 2005-P West Virginia: N/A **• 2005-D West Virginia:** N/A

Proof mintage (clad composition) • 2005-S West Virginia: N/A

Proof mintage (silver composition) • 2005-S West Virginia: N/A

2006 · NEVADA

State Treasure Brian Krolicki unveiled Nevada's design on June 2, 2005 after Nevada citizens cast their votes for a favorite design (at polling stations around the state, and on the Internet). The design, called "Morning in Nevada," features three wild mustangs running across the flatlands, with sagebrush branches and the Sierra Nevada Mountains providing scenery. A ribbon inscribed THE SILVER STATE emphasizes the importance of that precious metal to Nevada's history.

2006 · NEBRASKA

In 2003, John A. Gale, Nebraska secretary of state and chairman of the Nebraska Quarter Design Committee, called on Nebraskans to "show pride in their state by submitting a [state quarter] design." Submissions included a view of *The Sower*, a bronze statue on top of the state Capitol's tower; a view of the Capitol itself; and a portrait of Chief Standing Bear of the Ponca tribe. On June 1, 2005 Governor Dave Heineman announced the chosen design: a covered wagon with Chimney Rock in the background and the sun rising in the sky.

2006 · COLORADO

In the early months of 2004, Frances Owens, first lady of Colorado, began a tour to introduce schoolchildren and others to the state quarter concept, inviting designs to be submitted. Four of the five finalist designs featured the Rocky Mountains. On May 31, 2005, Governor Bill Owens announced that the Rockies will be the focus of the state's 2006 design. It features a majestic mountain backdrop above a banner with the legend COLORFUL COLORADO.

2006 · NORTH DAKOTA

In 2004, the North Dakota Quarter Design Commission began preparing written descriptions of suggested designs. The state's nine-member commission composed of historians, state politicians, educators, and tourism officials. More than 400 entries were received. In June 2005, the office of Governor John Hoeven announced that two grazing bison will be the focal point of the North Dakota state quarter. The design will also show the sun rising behind the buttes of the Badlands in southwestern North Dakota.

2006 · SOUTH DAKOTA

In April 2005, Governor Mike Rounds announced that South Dakota's state quarter will feature a view of Mount Rushmore flanked by single stalks of wheat and a Chinese ring-necked pheasant flying in the foreground. Rounds chose this design from five prospective choices recommended by the South Dakota Quarter Advisory Committee. Other motifs featured Mount Rushmore, American bison, and pheasants in various combinations.

2007 · MONTANA

Montana's new governor, Brian Schweitzer, was sworn into office January 3, 2005. He will develop a selection process for the state's quarter design. Montana's process will be similar to that of other states: design concepts will likely be solicited from the state's citizens; these will be narrowed down by a committee; and five motifs will be sent to the U.S. Mint for consideration.

2007 · WASHINGTON

Washington will go through a process similar to that of other states in its design selection. Design concepts will likely be solicited from Washington's citizens; then these will be narrowed down by a committee; and five motifs will be sent to the U.S. Mint for consideration.

2007 · IDAHO

Idaho will go through a process similar to that of other states in its design selection. Concepts will likely be solicited from Idaho's citizens; then these will be narrowed down by a committee; and five motifs will be sent to the U.S. Mint for consideration.

2007 · WYOMING

Wyoming citizens had until April 30, 2005 to submit ideas for the state's 2007 quarter. Submissions (through newspaper forms or the Internet) were to begin, "I think the back of the Wyoming quarter should show...." Governor Dave Freudenthal has appointed members to the Wyoming Coinage Advisory Committee.

2007 · UTAH

Former American Numismatic Association President H. Robert Campbell serves as chairman of the Utah quarter's Design Selection Committee. From the thousands of entries that will doubtless be received, Campbell's group will select 10 finalists to pass on to the commission and to the governor, who will then reduce the selection to five concepts to send to the U.S. Mint.

2008 · NEW MEXICO

New Mexico will go through a process similar to that of other states in its design selection. Design concepts will likely be solicited from New Mexico's citizens; then these will be narrowed down by a committee; and five motifs will be sent to the U.S. Mint for consideration.

2008 · ARIZONA

Arizona will go through a process similar to that of other states in its design selection. Concepts will likely be solicited from Arizona's citizens; then these will be narrowed down by a committee; and five motifs will be sent to the U.S. Mint for consideration.

2008 · ALASKA

Alaska will go through a process similar to that of other states in its design selection. Concepts will likely be solicited from Alaska's citizens; then these will be narrowed down by a committee; and five motifs will be sent to the U.S. Mint for consideration.

2008 · HAWAII

Hawaii will go through a process similar to that of other states in its design selection. Concepts will likely be solicited from Hawaii's citizens; then these will be narrowed down by a committee; and five motifs will be sent to the U.S. Mint for consideration.

DELAWARE THE FIRST STATE

Delaware became our 1st state on December 7, 1787. The ★ capital is Dover. Delaware gets its name from one of Virginia's early governors, Lord De La Warr. Delaware is the only state with no National Parks and is only nine miles wide at its narrowest point. Delaware's state bird, the Blue Hen Chicken, was chosen because, during the Revolutionary War, soldiers compared their military strength to that of these aggressive birds.

- CAPITAL... Dover
- STATE TREE... American Holly
- LAND AREA... 1,955 sq. mi.
- RANK IN SIZE (land area)... 49th
- STATE SONG... "Our Delaware"
- LARGEST CITY... Wilmington

BLUE HEN CHICKEN
PEACH BLOSSOM

STATE SEAL

STATE FLAG

PENNSYLVANIA SECOND STATE

Pennsylvania became our 2nd state on December 12, 1787. The ★ capital is Harrisburg. Pennsylvania was named for Admiral William Penn, father of the state's founder. Philadelphia was once the nation's capital. The first commercial radio broadcast originated from Pittsburgh. Pennsylvania was the birthplace of President James Buchanan as well as the first state to put its web site address on its license plates.

- CAPITAL... Harrisburg
- STATE TREE... Hemlock
- LAND AREA... 44,820 sq. mi.
- RANK IN SIZE (land area)... 32nd
- STATE SONG... "Pennsylvania"
- LARGEST CITY... Philadelphia

RUFFED GROUSE
MOUNTAIN LAUREL

STATE SEAL

STATE FLAG

NEW JERSEY GARDEN STATE

New Jersey became our 3rd state on December 18, 1787. The ★ capital is Trenton. New Jersey is one of the most crowded of the 50 states, with more than 1,000 people per square mile. It is the only state where every single county is classified as a metropolitan area. Vacation spot Atlantic City has the longest boardwalk in the world. New Jersey was the birthplace of President Grover Cleveland. Hungry for a burger? New Jersey is considered the diner capital of the world.

- CAPITAL...Trenton
- STATE TREE... Red Oak
- LAND AREA... 7,419 sq. mi.
- RANK IN SIZE (land area)... 46th
- STATE SONG... "Ode To New Jersey"
- LARGEST CITY... Newark

EASTERN GOLDFINCH
VIOLET

STATE SEAL

STATE FLAG

GEORGIA EMPIRE STATE OF THE SOUTH

Georgia became our 4th state on January 2, 1788. The ★ capital is Atlanta. Georgia is named after England's King George II. Georgia is the largest state east of the Mississippi and America's number one producer of peanuts and pecans. The first gold rush in the U.S. took place in northern Georgia in 1828 when gold was discovered near Dahlonega. Georgia is also the home state of President Jimmy Carter.

BROWN THRASHER
CHEROKEE ROSE

STATE SEAL

- CAPITAL... Atlanta
- STATE TREE... Live Oak
- LAND AREA... 57,919 sq. mi.
- RANK IN SIZE (land area)... 21st
- STATE SONG... "Georgia On My Mind"
- LARGEST CITY... Atlanta

STATE FLAG

CONNECTICUT CONSTITUTION STATE

Connecticut became our 5th state on January 9, 1788. The ★ capital is Hartford. Connecticut is an Algonquin and Mohican word meaning "place beside a long river." This place has produced some famous residents. Among them are circus pioneer P.T. Barnum, actress Katherine Hepburn, linguist Noah Webster, abolitionist John Brown, and President George W. Bush. The first atomic submarine was built in Connecticut. Our 5th state was one of only two states that never ratified the 18th amendment for prohibition.

ROBIN
MOUNTAIN LAUREL

STATE SEAL

- CAPITAL... Hartford
- STATE TREE... White Oak
- LAND AREA... 4,845 sq. mi.
- RANK IN SIZE (land area)... 48th
- STATE SONG... "Yankee Doodle"
- LARGEST CITY... Bridgeport

STATE FLAG

MASSACHUSETTS THE BAY STATE

Massachusetts became our 6th state on February 6, 1788. The ★ capital is Boston. In the Massachusett Indian language, the name meant "large hill place." Many presidents were born in Massachusetts: John Adams, John Quincy Adams, John F. Kennedy, and George Bush. Massachusetts also claims many firsts. The first subway was built in Boston in 1897; the first U.S. Postal code is Agawam, 01001; and Harvard was the first college in the country, founded in 1636. Of course, the state dessert is Boston Cream Pie.

CHICKADEE
MAYFLOWER

STATE SEAL

STATE FLAG

- CAPITAL... Boston
- STATE TREE... American Elm
- LAND AREA... 7,838 sq. mi.
- RANK IN SIZE (land area)... 45th
- STATE SONG... "All Hail to Massachusetts"
- LARGEST CITY... Boston

MARYLAND OLD LINE STATE

Maryland became our 7th state on April 28, 1788. The ★ capital is Annapolis, which once served as the capital of the United States. Maryland even gave up some of its land to help found Washington, D.C. The name Maryland was a tribute to Henrietta Maria, wife of King Charles I. Maryland is home to the U.S. Naval Academy and is the only state pronounced as a compound word. The state flag features the crests of Maryland's two founding families.

- CAPITAL... Annapolis
- STATE TREE... White Oak
- LAND AREA... 9,775 sq. mi.
- RANK IN SIZE (land area)... 42nd
- STATE SONG... "Maryland, My Maryland"
- LARGEST CITY... Baltimore

BALTIMORE ORIOLE
BLACK-EYED SUSAN

STATE SEAL

STATE FLAG

SOUTH CAROLINA PALMETTO STATE

South Carolina became our 8th state on May 23, 1788. The ★ capital is Columbia. Charleston, named after King Charles II, was the site of the first battle in the Civil War. President Andrew Jackson was born in South Carolina, which is also home to Upper Whitewater Falls, the highest waterfall in the east. The state flower is the Yellow Jessamine, and the state dance is none other than the Shag.

GREAT
CAROLINA WREN
YELLOW JESSAMINE

STATE SEAL

- CAPITAL... Columbia
- STATE TREE... Palmetto
- LAND AREA... 30,111 sq. mi.
- RANK IN SIZE (land area)... 40th
- STATE SONG... "Carolina"
- LARGEST CITY... Columbia

STATE FLAG

NEW HAMPSHIRE THE GRANITE STATE

New Hampshire became our 9th state on June 21, 1788. The ★ capital is Concord. Hampshire County was the English home of state co-founder Captain John Mason; this gives New Hampshire its name. New Hampshire was the first state to declare independence from England. Fittingly, the state motto is "Live Free or Die." President Franklin Pierce was born in New Hampshire.

- CAPITAL... Concord
- STATE TREE... White Birch
- LAND AREA... 8,969 sq. mi.
- RANK IN SIZE (land area)... 44th
- STATE SONG... "Old New Hampshire"
- LARGEST CITY... Manchester

PURPLE FINCH
PURPLE LILAC

STATE SEAL

STATE FLAG

VIRGINIA OLD DOMINION STATE

Virginia became our 10th state on June 25, 1788. The ★ capital is Richmond. Virginia got its name from England's "Virgin Queen," Elizabeth I. Jamestown was the first settlement in the United States. Two wars ended in Virginia: the American Revolution (when Cornwallis surrendered in Yorktown) and the Civil War (when Lee surrendered at Appomattox Courthouse). Eight American presidents were born in Virginia: George Washington, Thomas Jefferson, James Madison, James Monroe, William H. Harrison, John Tyler, Zachary Taylor, and Woodrow Wilson.

CARDINAL
DOGWOOD

STATE SEAL

STATE FLAG

- CAPITAL... Richmond
- STATE TREE... American Dogwood
- LAND AREA... 39,598 sq. mi.
- RANK IN SIZE (land area)... 37th
- STATE SONG... "Carry Me Back To Old Virginia"
- LARGEST CITY... Virginia Beach

NEW YORK EMPIRE STATE

New York became our 11th state on July 26, 1788. The ★ capital is Albany. New York is named after England's Duke of York. Four presidents were born in New York: Martin Van Buren, Millard Fillmore, Theodore Roosevelt, and Franklin Delano Roosevelt. The *New York Post* is the oldest running paper in the United States. There are more than 1,300 museums and galleries and 230 theaters in New York.

- CAPITAL… Albany
- STATE TREE… Sugar Maple
- LAND AREA… 47,224 sq. mi.
- RANK IN SIZE (land area)… 30th
- STATE SONG… "I Love New York"
- LARGEST CITY… New York City

BLUEBIRD
ROSE

STATE SEAL

STATE FLAG

NORTH CAROLINA THE TAR HEEL STATE

North Carolina became our 12th state on November 21, 1789. The ★ capital is Raleigh. This state was named after King Charles I. The nickname Tar Heel State originated during the Civil War when soldiers teased a cowardly regiment about needing tar to help them "stick it out" during battle. There are three mountain ranges in North Carolina: the Appalachian, the Blue Ridge, and the Great Smoky Mountains. Presidents James Polk and Andrew Johnson were born in North Carolina.

CARDINAL
AMERICAN DOGWOOD

STATE SEAL

- CAPITAL... Raleigh
- STATE TREE... Pine
- LAND AREA... 48,718 sq. mi.
- RANK IN SIZE (land area)... 29th
- STATE SONG... "The Old North State"
- LARGEST CITY... Charlotte

STATE FLAG

RHODE ISLAND THE OCEAN STATE

Rhode Island became our 13th state on May 29, 1790. The ★ capital is Providence. Our smallest state was named after the Dutch words for "red clay." Rhode Island made its political mark by refusing to ratify the U.S. Constitution without a Bill of Rights and by not ratifying the 18th amendment to the Constitution for prohibition. The state motto is Hope, the state flower is the Violet, and the state bird is the Rhode Island Red Hen.

- CAPITAL... Providence
- STATE TREE... Red Maple
- LAND AREA... 1,045 sq. mi.
- RANK IN SIZE (land area)... 50th
- STATE SONG... "Rhode Island, It's For Me"
- LARGEST CITY... Providence

RHODE ISLAND
RED HEN
VIOLET

STATE SEAL

STATE FLAG

★ VERMONT THE GREEN MOUNTAIN STATE

Vermont became our 14th state on March 4, 1791. The ★ capital is Montpelier. Vermont means "green mountain" in French. Two presidents were born in Vermont: Chester Arthur and Calvin Coolidge. Vermont was the first state admitted to the Union after the original 13 colonies. Vermont was also the first to outlaw slavery and the first U.S. patent was issued to a Vermonter.

**HERMIT THRUSH
RED CLOVER**

STATE SEAL

- CAPITAL... Montpelier
- STATE TREE... Sugar Maple
- LAND AREA... 9,249 sq. mi.
- RANK IN SIZE (land area)... 43rd
- STATE SONG... "These Green Mountains"
- LARGEST CITY... Burlington

STATE FLAG

KENTUCKY THE BLUEGRASS STATE

Kentucky became our 15th state on June 1, 1792. The ★ capital is Frankfort. Kentucky is an Iroquois word meaning "land of tomorrow." The state flag depicts two people acting out the state motto, "United We Stand, Divided We Fall." Kentucky is birthplace to U.S. President Abraham Lincoln and Confederate President Jefferson Davis. The oldest horse race in the country, the Kentucky Derby, takes place every year on the first Saturday in May.

- CAPITAL... Frankfort
- STATE TREE... Tulip Poplar
- LAND AREA... 39,732 sq. mi.
- RANK IN SIZE (land area)... 36th
- STATE SONG... "My Old
              Kentucky Home"
- LARGEST CITY... Louisville

CARDINAL
GOLDENROD

STATE SEAL

STATE FLAG

TENNESSEE THE VOLUNTEER STATE

Tennessee became our 16th state on June 1, 1796. The ★ capital is Nashville. Tennessee is taken from "tanasi," the Cherokee word for "villages." The Grand Ole Opry is the longest running live radio program in the country, broadcast every week since 1925. The nickname, Volunteer State, was given because of the bravery of Tennessee's volunteer soldiers in the Battle of New Orleans in the War of 1812.

- CAPITAL... Nashville
- STATE TREE... Tulip Poplar
- LAND AREA... 41,220 sq. mi.
- RANK IN SIZE (land area)... 34th
- STATE SONG... "The Tennessee Waltz"
- LARGEST CITY... Memphis

MOCKINGBIRD
IRIS

STATE SEAL

STATE FLAG

OHIO THE BUCKEYE STATE

Ohio became our 17th state on March 1, 1803. The ★ capital is Columbus. Ohio, which means "good river" in Iroquois, is the birthplace of seven presidents: Grant, Hayes, Garfield, B. Harrison, McKinley, Taft, and Harding. Ohio gave us the first traffic light (1923), the first cash register (1878), and the first hot dog (1900). Interestingly, Ohioans have made their mark in space: Neil Armstrong was the first man to walk on the moon and John Glenn is the oldest man to fly in outer space to date.

- CAPITAL... Columbus
- STATE TREE... Buckeye
- LAND AREA... 40,953 sq. mi.
- RANK IN SIZE (land area)... 35th
- STATE SONG... "Beautiful Ohio"
- LARGEST CITY... Columbus

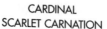

CARDINAL
SCARLET CARNATION

STATE SEAL

STATE FLAG

LOUISIANA THE PELICAN STATE

Louisiana became our 18th state on April 30, 1812. The ★ capital is Baton Rouge. Louisiana is named in honor of King Louis XIV and is the only state in the Union that has parishes instead of counties. Because of slow communication, the famous Battle of New Orleans was actually fought two weeks after the War of 1812 ended. Louisiana is one of the most racially and culturally diverse states, with French, Spanish, Cuban, and African influences.

EASTERN BROWN
PELICAN
MAGNOLIA

STATE SEAL

- CAPITAL... Baton Rouge
- STATE TREE... Bald Cypress
- LAND AREA... 43,566 sq. mi.
- RANK IN SIZE (land area)... 33rd
- STATE SONG... "Give Me Louisiana"
- LARGEST CITY... New Orleans

STATE FLAG

INDIANA THE HOOSIER STATE

Indiana became our 19th state on December 11, 1816. The ★ capital is Indianapolis. The name of this state was created by Congress to symbolize the "land of the Indians." Indiana's official motto is The Crossroads of America, and it's known as the Hoosier State, a phrase associated with athletics but actually taken from a poem written in the 1930s.

- CAPITAL... Indianapolis
- STATE TREE... Tulip Tree
- LAND AREA... 35,870 sq. mi.
- RANK IN SIZE (land area)... 38th
- STATE SONG... "On The Banks of the Wabash"
- LARGEST CITY... Indianapolis

CARDINAL
PEONY

STATE SEAL

STATE FLAG

MISSISSIPPI THE MAGNOLIA STATE

Mississippi became our 20th state on December 10, 1817. The ★ capital is Jackson. The name derives from the Chippewa words "mmici zibi," meaning "Father of Waters." The first lung and heart transplants were performed in Mississippi. Memorial Day was first celebrated in 1866 at the Friendship Cemetery in Columbus when the women of the town decorated both Union and Confederate graves to remember the dead.

MOCKINGBIRD
MAGNOLIA

STATE SEAL

- CAPITAL… Jackson
- STATE TREE… Magnolia
- LAND AREA… 46,914 sq. mi.
- RANK IN SIZE (land area)… 31st
- STATE SONG… "Go Mississippi"
- LARGEST CITY… Jackson

STATE FLAG

ILLINOIS THE LAND OF LINCOLN

Illinois became our 21st state on December 3, 1818. The ★ capital is Springfield. Illinois is an Algonquin word meaning "tribe of superior men." Illinois was the first state to ratify the 13th Amendment abolishing slavery. The tallest skyscraper in North America is the Sears Tower in Chicago. Illinois is the birthplace of President Ronald Reagan.

- CAPITAL... Springfield
- STATE TREE... White Oak
- LAND AREA... 55,593 sq. mi.
- RANK IN SIZE (land area)... 24th
- STATE SONG... "Illinois"
- LARGEST CITY... Chicago

CARDINAL
PURPLE VIOLET

STATE SEAL

STATE FLAG

ALABAMA THE YELLOWHAMMER STATE

Alabama became our 22nd state on December 14, 1819. The ★ capital is Montgomery. In the Creek Indian language, Alabama means "tribal town." The state nickname, Yellowhammer State, dates back to the Civil War and refers to the new, bright yellow cloth that was used on soldiers' uniforms. Famous Alabamians include baseball player Hank Aaron and educator Helen Keller.

YELLOWHAMMER
CAMELLIA

STATE SEAL

- CAPITAL… Montgomery
- STATE TREE… Southern Pine
- LAND AREA… 50,750 sq. mi.
- RANK IN SIZE (land area)… 28th
- STATE SONG… "Alabama"
- LARGEST CITY… Birmingham

STATE FLAG

MAINE THE PINE TREE STATE

Maine became our 23rd state on March 15, 1820. The ★ capital is Augusta. Maine is a reference to the "main land," as opposed to the off-shore islands of that region. Maine is the only state with a one-syllable name and the only state that borders just one other state. Maine has so many deep harbors that all the navies in the world could drop anchor in them.

- CAPITAL... Augusta
- STATE TREE... White Pine
- LAND AREA... 30,865 sq. mi.
- RANK IN SIZE (land area)... 39th
- STATE SONG... "State of
                        Maine Song"
- LARGEST CITY... Portland

CHICKADEE
WHITE PINE CONE
AND TASSEL

STATE SEAL

STATE FLAG

MISSOURI THE SHOW ME STATE

Missouri became our 24th state on August 10, 1821. The ★ capital is Jefferson City. Missouri is an Indian word meaning "town of large canoes." The Pony Express began in Missouri in 1860. Ice cream was invented at the 1904 World's Fair in Missouri. Harry S Truman was born in Missouri, as was TV newscaster Walter Cronkite, entertainment visionary Walt Disney, and novelist Mark Twain.

**BLUEBIRD
HAWTHORN**

STATE SEAL

- CAPITAL... Jefferson City
- STATE TREE... Flowering Dogwood
- LAND AREA... 68,898 sq. mi.
- RANK IN SIZE (land area)... 18th
- STATE SONG... "Missouri Waltz"
- LARGEST CITY... Kansas City

STATE FLAG

ARKANSAS THE NATURAL STATE

Arkansas became our 25th state on June 15th, 1836. The ★ capital is Little Rock.

The state gets its name from a Sioux word "acansa," meaning "downstream place."

The Arkansas flag sports a red diamond, representing that it is the only state in the nation where diamonds are actively mined. President Bill Clinton was born in Arkansas. To end the pronunciation debate, in 1881, the General Assembly resolved that Arkan-SAW is the correct way to say this state's name.

MOCKINGBIRD APPLE BLOSSOM   STATE SEAL

- CAPITAL... Little Rock
- STATE TREE... Pine
- LAND AREA... 52,075 sq. mi.
- RANK IN SIZE (land area)... 27th
- STATE SONG... "Arkansas, Oh, Arkansas"
- LARGEST CITY... Little Rock

STATE FLAG

MICHIGAN THE WOLVERINE STATE

Michigan became our 26th state on January 26th, 1837. The ★ capital is Lansing. The state gets its name from the Chippewa word "meicigana," meaning "great or large lake." Michigan has the largest of the Great Lakes. Michigan was the first state to guarantee every child in the state the right to a high school education.

ROBIN
APPLE BLOSSOM

STATE SEAL

- CAPITAL... Lansing
- STATE TREE... White Pine
- LAND AREA... 56,809 sq. mi.
- RANK IN SIZE (land area)... 22nd
- STATE SONG... "Michigan, My Michigan"
- LARGEST CITY... Detroit

STATE FLAG

FLORIDA THE SUNSHINE STATE

Florida became our 27th state on March 3, 1845. The ★ capital is Tallahassee. Explorer Ponce de Leon named Florida after the Pasqua de Flores, or "feast of flowers," that he celebrated on Easter, 1531. Even though people call Florida the Sunshine State, its real nickname is the Orange State because it is the nation's largest orange grower. It is also the place to go to see space launches from Cape Canaveral.

- CAPITAL... Tallahassee
- STATE TREE... Sabal Palmetto
- LAND AREA... 53,997 sq. mi.
- RANK IN SIZE (land area)... 26th
- STATE SONG... "Suwannee River"
- LARGEST CITY... Jacksonville

MOCKINGBIRD
ORANGE BLOSSOM

STATE SEAL

STATE FLAG

TEXAS THE LONE STAR STATE

Texas became our 28th state on December 29, 1845. The ★ capital is Austin. The name Texas comes from the word "tejas," meaning "friends and allies." Notable in Texas state history is that from 1836 to 1845 Texas was an independent nation. Today Texas claims 7.4% of the total area of the United States, making it the second largest state. Presidents Dwight D. Eisenhower and Lyndon B. Johnson were born in the Lone Star State.

- CAPITAL... Austin
- STATE TREE... Pecan
- LAND AREA... 261,914 sq. mi.
- RANK IN SIZE (land area)... 2nd
- STATE SONG... "Texas, Our Texas"
- LARGEST CITY... Houston

MOCKINGBIRD
BLUEBONNET

STATE SEAL

STATE FLAG

IOWA THE HAWKEYE STATE

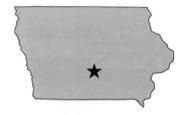

Iowa became our 29th state on December 28, 1846. The ★ capital is Des Moines. Iowa is from the Indian word "ayuxwa," meaning "one who soothes." President Herbert Hoover, a native Iowan, was the first president born west of the Mississippi. Iowa has a beautiful state rock, the geode. It's found in limestone nodules and when broken open reveals a lining of colorful quartz and crystals.

- CAPITAL… Des Moines
- STATE TREE… Oak
- LAND AREA… 55,875 sq. mi.
- RANK IN SIZE (land area)… 23rd
- STATE SONG… "The Song of Iowa"
- LARGEST CITY… Des Moines

EASTERN GOLDFINCH
WILD PRAIRIE ROSE

STATE SEAL

STATE FLAG

WISCONSIN THE BADGER STATE

Wisconsin became our 30th state on May 29, 1848. The ★ capital is Madison.

In the Chippewa tongue, Wisconsin means "a grassy place." Wisconsin is the nation's leading milk producer. Over 1.5 million cows give enough milk to supply 42 million people for a year; that's not counting butter or cheese. The first kindergarten in the nation was started in Wisconsin in 1856.

- CAPITAL... Madison
- STATE TREE... Sugar Maple
- LAND AREA... 54,314 sq. mi.
- RANK IN SIZE (land area)... 25th
- STATE SONG... "On Wisconsin"
- LARGEST CITY... Milwaukee

ROBIN
WOOD VIOLET

STATE SEAL

STATE FLAG

CALIFORNIA THE GOLDEN STATE

California became our 31st state on September 9, 1850. The ★ capital is Sacramento. California was named after a mythical Spanish paradise. California's motto is Eureka, which translates as "I have found it!"—a perfect slogan for the gold rush. In Sequoia National Park there is a 3,500-year-old Redwood, and California's Mt. Whitney is the highest peak in the "lower 48." President Richard Nixon was born in California.

- CAPITAL... Sacramento
- STATE TREE... California Redwood
- LAND AREA... 155,973 sq. mi.
- RANK IN SIZE (land area)... 3rd
- STATE SONG... "I Love You, California"
- LARGEST CITY... Los Angeles

CALIFORNIA VALLEY
QUAIL
GOLDEN POPPY

STATE SEAL

STATE FLAG

MINNESOTA THE GOPHER STATE

Minnesota became our 32nd state on May 11, 1858. The ★ capital is St. Paul. Minnesota is Sioux for "sky-tinted water." Be careful; it's illegal to pick the state flower, a Pink and White Lady's-Slipper. Minnesotan baseball commentator Halsey Hal was the first to say "Holy Cow" in a broadcast. Many inventions have come from Minnesota including Scotch tape, HMOs, the stapler, and the bundt pan.

COMMON LOON
PINK and WHITE
LADY'S-SLIPPER

STATE SEAL

- CAPITAL... St. Paul
- STATE TREE... Norway Pine
- LAND AREA... 79,617 sq. mi.
- RANK IN SIZE (land area)... 14th
- STATE SONG... "Hail! Minnesota"
- LARGEST CITY... Minneapolis

STATE FLAG

OREGON THE BEAVER STATE

Oregon became our 33rd state on February 14, 1859. The ★ capital is Salem. The origin of the word Oregon is unknown. Oregon is the only state with a flag that has two designs. The reverse side has a picture of a beaver. The deepest lake in the United States is Oregon's Crater Lake, formed by an ancient volcano. Another Oregon claim to fame is ghost towns—it has more than any other state.

- CAPITAL... Salem
- STATE TREE... Douglas Fir
- LAND AREA... 96,003 sq. mi.
- RANK IN SIZE (land area)... 10th
- STATE SONG... "Oregon, My Oregon"
- LARGEST CITY... Portland

WESTERN MEADOWLARK
OREGON GRAPE

STATE SEAL

STATE FLAG

KANSAS THE SUNFLOWER STATE

Kansas became our 34th state on January 29, 1861. The ★ capital is Topeka. The state name originated from an Indian word, "konza," meaning "people of the south wind." A Kansas county is the geographical center of the United States. Kansan Hattie McDaniel was the first African-American woman to win an Academy Award. The first woman mayor in the U.S. was elected in Kansas in 1887.

WESTERN
MEADOWLARK
SUNFLOWER

STATE SEAL

- CAPITAL... Topeka
- STATE TREE... Cottonwood
- LAND AREA... 81,823 sq. mi.
- RANK IN SIZE (land area)... 13th
- STATE SONG... "Home
  on the Range"
- LARGEST CITY... Wichita

STATE FLAG

111

WEST VIRGINIA THE MOUNTAIN STATE

West Virginia became our 35th state on June 20, 1863. The ★ capital is Charleston. This state takes its name from the "Virgin Queen," Elizabeth I.

Mother's Day began in West Virginia and that's just one of many firsts. The first rural mail delivery, the first brick street, the first major battle of the Civil War, the first free school for African Americans, and the first state sales tax all originated in the Mountain State.

- CAPITAL... Charleston
- STATE TREE... Sugar Maple
- LAND AREA... 24,087 sq. mi.
- RANK IN SIZE (land area)... 41st
- STATE SONG... "The West Virginia Hills"
- LARGEST CITY... Huntington (Metropolitan Area)

CARDINAL RHODODENDRON

STATE SEAL

STATE FLAG

NEVADA THE SILVER STATE

TO BE RELEASED IN 2006

Nevada became our 36th state on October 31, 1864. The ★ capital is Carson City. Nevada means "snow capped" in Spanish. Nevada produces the most gold in the nation. The Nevada constitution was sent by telegram in Morse code from Carson City to Washington, D.C. in 1864. The transmission took hours. There are more hotel rooms in Las Vegas than anywhere else in the world.

MOUNTAIN BLUEBIRD
SAGEBRUSH

STATE SEAL

- CAPITAL... Carson City
- STATE TREE... Bristlecone Pine/ Single Leaf Piñon
- LAND AREA... 109,806 sq. mi.
- RANK IN SIZE (land area)... 7th
- STATE SONG... "Home Means Nevada"
- LARGEST CITY... Las Vegas

STATE FLAG

NEBRASKA THE CORNHUSKER STATE

TO BE RELEASED IN 2006

Nebraska became our 37th state on March 1, 1867. The ★ capital is Lincoln. Nebraska gets its name from an Oto Indian word meaning "flat water." President Gerald Ford was born in the Cornhusker State, which is not a reference to hard farm work, but to the University of Nebraska athletic teams. The 911 emergency calling system was developed in Nebraska.

- CAPITAL... Lincoln
- STATE TREE... Cottonwood
- LAND AREA... 76,878 sq. mi.
- RANK IN SIZE (land area)... 15th
- STATE SONG... "Beautiful Nebraska"
- LARGEST CITY... Omaha

WESTERN MEADOWLARK
GOLDENROD

STATE SEAL

STATE FLAG

COLORADO THE CENTENNIAL STATE

TO BE RELEASED IN 2006

Colorado became our 38th state on August 1, 1876. The ★ capital is Denver. Colorado was originally a Spanish reference to the red rock around the Colorado River. The federal government owns one-third of the land in Colorado. This was the only state to ever turn down the opportunity to host an Olympics (1976). The United States Air Force Academy is located in Colorado.

LARK BUNTING
WHITE & LAVENDER
COLUMBINE

STATE SEAL

- CAPITAL... Denver
- STATE TREE... Colorado Blue Spruce
- LAND AREA... 103,729 sq. mi.
- RANK IN SIZE (land area)... 8th
- STATE SONG... "Where The Columbines Grow"
- LARGEST CITY... Denver

STATE FLAG

NORTH DAKOTA THE FLICKERTAIL STATE

TO BE RELEASED IN 2006

North Dakota became our 39th state on November 2 1889. The ★ capital is Bismarck. Dakota is a Sioux word meaning "allies." The town of Rugby is the geographical center of the North American continent. The state legislature has twice tried to change the name of the state with no success. Before he was president, Theodore Roosevelt fought with a North Dakota regiment in the Spanish-American War.

- CAPITAL… Bismarck
- STATE TREE… American Elm
- LAND AREA… 68,994 sq. mi.
- RANK IN SIZE (land area)… 17th
- STATE SONG… "North Dakota Hymn"
- LARGEST CITY… Fargo

WESTERN MEADOWLARK
WILD PRAIRIE ROSE

STATE SEAL

STATE FLAG

SOUTH DAKOTA MOUNT RUSHMORE STATE

TO BE RELEASED IN 2006

South Dakota became our 40th state on November 2, 1889. The ★ capital is Pierre. Mt. Rushmore is in South Dakota, as is the prairie that was made famous in the Little House books by Laura Ingalls Wilder. Outlaw Jesse James once escaped capture by jumping a 20-foot chasm at Devil's Gulch. News anchor Tom Brokaw was born and raised in South Dakota.

RING-NECKED
PHEASANT
PASQUE FLOWER

STATE SEAL

- CAPITAL... Pierre
- STATE TREE... Black Hills Spruce
- LAND AREA... 75,896 sq. mi.
- RANK IN SIZE (land area)... 16th
- STATE SONG... "Hail South Dakota"
- LARGEST CITY... Sioux Falls

STATE FLAG

MONTANA THE TREASURE STATE

TO BE
RELEASED
IN 2007

Montana became our 41st state on November 8, 1889. The ★ capital is Helena. Montana is the Spanish word for "mountainous." Antelope, elk, and deer outnumber Montana's two-legged residents. The world's shortest river, the Roe River, runs a whopping 200 feet across the state. A famous landmark is Little Bighorn, where the Sioux and Cheyenne defeated General Custer.

- CAPITAL... Helena
- STATE TREE... Ponderosa Pine
- LAND AREA... 145,556 sq. mi.
- RANK IN SIZE (land area)... 4th
- STATE SONG... "Montana"
- LARGEST CITY... Billings

WESTERN
MEADOWLARK
BITTERROOT

STATE SEAL

STATE FLAG

WASHINGTON THE EVERGREEN STATE

TO BE
RELEASED
IN 2007

Washington became our 42nd state on November 11, 1889. The ★ capital is Olympia. Washington is named after George Washington and is the only state named after a president. The first revolving restaurant made its debut in Seattle. More than half the apples eaten in the U.S. are grown in Washington orchards. Washington has more glaciers than all the other "lower 48" states combined.

WILLOW
GOLDFINCH
COAST
RHODODENDRON

STATE SEAL

- CAPITAL... Olympia
- STATE TREE... Western Hemlock
- LAND AREA... 66,581 sq. mi.
- RANK IN SIZE (land area)... 20th
- STATE SONG... "Washington, My Home"
- LARGEST CITY... Seattle

STATE FLAG

IDAHO THE GEM STATE

Idaho became our 43rd state on July 3, 1890. The ★ capital is Boise. The meaning of the name Idaho is unknown. A U.S. citizen made it up. Idaho is the nation's number one producer of potatoes. The deepest river gorge in North America is Hell's Canyon, deeper than even the Grand Canyon. Television was invented in Idaho in 1926. Idaho is the home state of Olympic Gold Medalist skier Picabo Street.

- CAPITAL... Boise
- STATE TREE... Western White Pine
- LAND AREA... 82,751 sq. mi.
- RANK IN SIZE (land area)... 11th
- STATE SONG... "Here We Have Idaho"
- LARGEST CITY... Boise

MOUNTAIN BLUEBIRD
SYRINGA

STATE SEAL

STATE FLAG

WYOMING THE EQUALITY STATE

TO BE
RELEASED
IN 2007

Wyoming became our 44th state on July 10, 1890. The ★ capital is Cheyenne. Wyoming was named by combining two Indian words meaning "at the big flats." This was the first state to give women the right to vote. Yellowstone was the first National Park, and Devil's Tower was the first National Monument. Wyoming is the least populated state in the country.

WESTERN
MEADOWLARK
INDIAN PAINTBRUSH

STATE SEAL

- CAPITAL... Cheyenne
- STATE TREE... Cottonwood
- LAND AREA... 97,105 sq. mi.
- RANK IN SIZE (land area)... 9th
- STATE SONG... "Wyoming"
- LARGEST CITY... Cheyenne

STATE FLAG

UTAH THE BEEHIVE STATE

TO BE
RELEASED
IN 2007

Utah became our 45th state on January 4, 1896. The ★ capital is Salt Lake City. Utah comes from an Ute Indian word meaning "people of the mountains." Utah's average peak elevation is the highest in the U.S. The first transcontinental railway was completed in Utah in 1869. Tools dating back 10,000 years have been found in caves in the Utah foothills. Utah's Great Salt Lake, 92 miles long and 48 miles wide, is the largest salt lake in this hemisphere.

- CAPITAL... Salt Lake City
- STATE TREE... Blue Spruce
- LAND AREA... 82,168 sq. mi.
- RANK IN SIZE (land area)... 12th
- STATE SONG... "Utah We Love Thee"
- LARGEST CITY... Salt Lake City

AMERICAN SEAGULL
SEGO LILY

STATE SEAL

STATE FLAG

OKLAHOMA THE SOONER STATE

TO BE RELEASED IN 2008

Oklahoma became our 46th state on November 16, 1907. The ★ capital is Oklahoma City. Oklahoma gets its name from Indian words meaning "red person." There are 12 different ecosystems in Oklahoma including mesas, wetlands, sand dunes, and prairies. Two inventions that come from Oklahoma are the shopping cart and the parking meter.

SCISSOR-TAILED FLYCATCHER MISTLETOE

STATE SEAL

- CAPITAL... Oklahoma City
- STATE TREE... Redbud
- LAND AREA... 68,679 sq. mi.
- RANK IN SIZE (land area)... 19th
- STATE SONG... "Oklahoma"
- LARGEST CITY... Oklahoma City

STATE FLAG

NEW MEXICO LAND OF ENCHANTMENT

TO BE RELEASED IN 2008

New Mexico became our 47th state on January 6, 1912. The ★ capital is Santa Fe. New Mexico is named from Spanish words meaning "lands north of the Rio Grande." Santa Fe, elevation 7,000 feet, is the highest capital city in the U.S. The world's first atomic bomb was developed in Los Alamos. New Mexico's state flower, the Yucca Plant, can be used for soap and its leaves as a needle and thread. The state bird is the Roadrunner.

- CAPITAL... Santa Fe
- STATE TREE... Piñon Pine
- LAND AREA... 121,365 sq. mi.
- RANK IN SIZE (land area)... 5th
- STATE SONG... "O, Fair
                  New Mexico"
- LARGEST CITY... Albuquerque

ROADRUNNER
YUCCA FLOWER

STATE SEAL

STATE FLAG

ARIZONA THE GRAND CANYON STATE

CACTUS WREN
SAGUARO
CACTUS BLOSSOM

STATE SEAL

STATE FLAG

TO BE RELEASED IN 2008

Arizona became our 48th state on February 14, 1912. The ★ capital is Phoenix. Arizona is the Spanish interpretation of Aztec words meaning "silver bearing." About 550 million years ago, Arizona was under water. As the water receded, it created natural wonders like the Grand Canyon. Today, there are four deserts in Arizona: the Sorrow, Mojave, Great Basin, and Chihuahua.

- CAPITAL... Phoenix
- STATE TREE... Palo Verde
- LAND AREA... 111,642 sq. mi.
- RANK IN SIZE (land area)... 6th
- STATE SONG... "Arizona March Song"
- LARGEST CITY... Phoenix

ALASKA THE LAST FRONTIER

TO BE RELEASED IN 2008

Alaska became our 49th state on January 3, 1959. The ★ capital is Juneau. Eskimo words meaning "great lands" give Alaska its name. Alaska has 33,904 square miles of shoreline, more than any other state. Alaska also has more than 100 State Parks and four different climate zones: maritime, arctic, continental, and transitional. During summer in Barrow, Alaska, the sun doesn't set for 84 days.

- CAPITAL... Juneau
- STATE TREE... Sitka Spruce
- LAND AREA... 570,374 sq. mi.
- RANK IN SIZE (land area)... 1st
- STATE SONG... "Alaska's Flag"
- LARGEST CITY... Anchorage

WILLOW PTARMIGAN
FORGET ME NOT

STATE SEAL

STATE FLAG

HAWAII THE ALOHA STATE

TO BE
RELEASED
IN 2008

Hawaii became our 50th state on August 21, 1959. The ★ capital is Honolulu. The name Hawaii is probably based on the Hawaiian word for "volcanic homeland." Hawaii was an island kingdom until Captain Cook claimed it for Britain in 1775. There are only 12 letters in the Hawaiian alphabet. Although Hawaii is not connected to any other state, it somehow manages to have three interstate highways.

NENE
PUA ALOALO

STATE SEAL

- CAPITAL... Honolulu
- STATE TREE... Kukui Candlenut
- LAND AREA... 6,423 sq. mi.
- RANK IN SIZE (land area)... 47th
- STATE SONG... "Hawaii Ponoi"
- LARGEST CITY... Honolulu

STATE FLAG

COIN SPECIFICATIONS
FOR ALL STATE QUARTERS, 1999 TO DATE

Circulation and Proof strike mintages: Given individually in the preceding pages.

Designed by (obverse): Originally designed by John Flanagan, whose initials JF are on the neck truncation. The appearance of the portrait was vastly altered by William Cousins in 1999, by adding extensive hair details. In that year the initials WC were added to those of Flanagan, now appearing run together as JFWC. The W is of unusual appearance and is not easily recognizable as such. Likely, this should be called the Cousins portrait of Washington, rather than a portrait by either Houdon or Flanagan.

Specifications (clad issues):
- *Composition:* Outer layers of copper-nickel (75% copper and 25% nickel) bonded to an inner core of pure copper. The copper is visible when the coin is viewed edge-on.
- *Diameter:* 24.3 mm
- *Weight:* 87.5 grains
- *Edge:* Reeded

Specifications (silver issues):
- *Composition:* 90% silver; 10% copper
- *Diameter:* 24.3 mm
- *Weight:* 96.45 grains
- *Edge:* Reeded